MS. TIFFANY'S
PALM BEACH

Above Stairs to Below Stairs

By

PAULINE TIFFANY,
M.S., MHCI, GREAT BRITAIN

White Horse Publishing

ISBN: 978-0-9706651-2-6

Library of Congress Cataloging-in-Publication Data
is available on file.

Printed in the United States by Morris Publishing®
3212 East Highway 30
Kearney, NE 68847
1-800-650-7888

MS. TIFFANY'S PALM BEACH

PREFACE

My extraordinary life, going from *Above Stairs,* if you will, from the Halls of Parliament, International Diplomacy, childhood friends of Prince Michael and Richard, children of the Duke and Duchess of Gloucester, to the *Below Stairs* world of Palm Beach staff.

I was the private Chef for David Gilmour, owner of the Island of Wakaya where he produced Fiji Water, and also happens to be the world's largest miner of gold. I first met Barbara Taylor Bradford, the famous fiction writer, when she dined at the Gilmours, along with Presidents, Royalty and Movie Stars.

There is a chapter about my being Chef and Estate Manager for rock star Rod Stewart and his model wife, Rachel Hunter, in their Palm Beach home.

I was privileged to manage well-known Palm Beach Restaurants and meeting the Who's Who of the Disney World for the rich.

I put estates together (worth millions) for their famous owners, outfitting them with all the necessary equipment for their dining rooms and kitchens. Being originally in that world (but now part of the staff), I understood what was required to impress their friends and business associates.

Teaching the first Culinary Arts Chef's Program, as a certified teacher, (long before the Culinary Institute of America was even thought of, I believe that I broke the "glass ceiling", being a woman of the sixties in a man's domain.

I owned one of the Top 100 restaurants in Florida, winning so many awards, had a Cooking School, live TV show and made videos on Catering.

You will go along with me and see how, at the age of thirteen, I was to become involved, with my family, in a political adventure to Czechoslovakia. My father, Stanley Tiffany, M.P., C.B.E., had met Jan Masaryk, who was the Foreign Minister of the country, just a few months before. Shortly after Father returned back to England, Jan Masaryk was murdered by communist agents trying to take over his country of Czechoslovakia.

There are many more interesting, and fun chapters in the book. By the way, I have included some "juicy scandals" that will "tickle your fancies." This is not a cookbook, but I have included some of the easy to prepare favorite recipes of my employers, plus menu information dating back to the sixties.

I have lived with these Palm Beach people, laughed and cried with them, being a part of their family life. Such unusual happenings that you would think this book is fiction ~ but I assure you, it is all true.

Pauline Tiffany, M.S., M.H.C.I. (Great Britain)

MS. TIFFANY'S PALM BEACH

INTRODUCTION

Here I was on my way headed north to my sister's home on Florida's Space Coast in the old Lincoln Mercury, which reminded me of Coleman's dry mustard from Norwich, England. I always felt the same way about the car because Dick bought it second-hand ten years before, so now it is more like a tin of caked dry mustard than a fresh aromatic one. I stand corrected... by then it was plenty aromatic. If cars could have feelings, then this one was protesting loudly.

With the oppressive July heat wave, it sputtered and choked, delivering blasts of warm and frigid air. Perhaps the car was protesting so much because it was laden down with my belongings. I had things that I needed for my future use. My sons moved the rest of my things to a new storage unit, at least what was left of them.

A suitcase full of cookbooks including *Le Repertoire de La Cuisine* (the Chef's bible), recipes from my cooking school and two copies of each of my videos on *Profitable Catering Made Easy*, along with all of my black dresses, chef whites, and of course the Hobart K5A mixer, that Julia Childs and I both agree is an extension of the chef's soul, were crammed into the back seat. As for me, I was shaking as bad as the car's air conditioner, plus I only had eighteen dollars in my purse. What normally takes two hours to get to my sister's home, now took me three hours as I had to pull over to the side of the road to have a quiet sob.

The enormity of my actions began just twenty-four hours before when I was in the library, and it hit me like a jack hammer. How did I suddenly realize I was abused? There I was to get a list of colleges and culinary schools that I could send information to, regarding my catering videos. On the table was a very small book called *The Emotionally Abused Woman.* I opened up the book, read it and realized I was that woman.

I hurried home... never my house... always his house, in his name only, not mine. I told my boys the whole truth. My boys did not realize that I was abused mentally and later I told them there was some physical abuse, but the mental abuse was the most destructive... I had lied to them.

With all my money gone and all my worldly goods distributed into three different storage units, only one that I had knowledge of, and a key, not that it made any difference to me as *I did not care less.*

I don't remember the whole trip but I made it to my sister's home, emotionally drained but she was ready for me with a good cup of Yorkshire tea. I knew I had to get a divorce and file for bankruptcy.

Dick had maxed out all of my credit cards that I had obtained as a single woman when I was making a good income. He would, unbeknownst to me, go to the Fort Lauderdale International Airport where he could withdraw more money than a regular A.T.M. machine.

I knew that to pay for these things, I would have to sell or pawn what jewelry I had left. Apparently someone had broken into the house before I left and had stolen my jewelry, but did not touch his watches or his other valuables left in the same drawer. Later on, my youngest son (who was well-entrenched in the county fire service), informed me that the police believed that Dick was involved after he had refused to take a lie-detector test. I still at that time had my blinders on. Of course, soon the "penny would drop", as they say in England.

My sister and I put my resume together with the album of my life that my mother had done when visiting me. Mother used copies of my degrees, diplomas, and photographs that would be most useful to show my talents for employment. I needed to find a job with accommodations, but in my sister's area there were no such opportunities. I soon realized that I must leave this safe haven and head south. I had worked in Palm Beach before so I knew the area and the type of people that could utilize my multifaceted talents.

At last, no longer would I be forbidden to have friends and family close to me. He would no longer be the center of attention from the newspapers and magazines, pushing me aside to take all of the accolades, as I had to make sure that he was known as the Owner and I, the manager, of a restaurant business (when he did not known what was on the menu or the wine list). No more would I be "on stage" having to watch every word I uttered, in case I said the wrong thing. Now I could breathe freely... Oh the joy of being alive.

What I am about to tell you, in my book, will "knock the socks off" most of my contemporaries, and I assure you this as my Mother would say, "this is not a fairy story" – a nice way of saying no lies.

So let me begin to enlighten you on the true story of Pauline Tiffany.

MS. TIFFANY'S PALM BEACH

Chapter

1 BIRTH, WAR AND PEACE

It was not at all unusual to have cold and wet weather in Yorkshire, and on December 10th in 1936, it was a corker. Everybody stayed indoors and wrapped up, even young schoolboys who wore the regulation short pants and knee socks, which toughened them up and froze their knees. But everybody was glued to the radio. You see, the King was coming on the radio to announce to his people that he was going to abdicate the throne to marry Mrs. Wallis Simpson, an American divorcee. The whole nation was talking about this news except my mother, who was at home in labor giving birth to me, my parents' first child. Yes, an historic event and I shared the date. Little did I know that many years later, I would meet the Duke and Duchess of Windsor in Palm Beach, Florida.

My father, born and educated in Leeds, followed an electrical engineer profession at the Walter Haigh Coal Mine. My grandfather Tiffany was already deceased and my grandmother Tiffany had been rejected by her wealthy family, disinherited and shunned because she fell in love and married my grandfather.

Things were about to change with my father's work because the war was on our doorstep. Father was called to take his physical for the army but the Minister of Labour stepped in and said, "Aha! Here is Tiffany, an electrical engineer, can't have him in khaki!" and almost before he knew what was happening, he was back home in Leeds and found himself pinned down for the rest of the war in the Royal Ordinance factory in Barnbow.

My father was interested in politics and was voted in as Head Director of Leeds Industrial Co-Operative Society Ltd. in

Albion Street in Leeds. There were lots of these stores, all over the country, which were just like big supermarkets in the U.S.A. and each member had a number that was used when they wanted to make purchases (I remember our number was 106639).

In 1938, two years after I was born, they had a new extension added onto the building and when you walked through the front doors, there was a "lift" (elevator) with a big sign above it that had my father's name on it. And, in the restaurant on the fourth floor was a beautiful walnut high chair with a bronze plaque on the back of it with my name on it. The Co-operative Society would become a big factor in my father's political career.

On Sunday, September 3, 1939 - War was declared by Neville Chamberlain, who was Prime Minister at the time. He declared we were at war with Germany. They had taken over Poland and Czechoslovakia and now we were to get ready to fight Hitler. We were on our own at this time because the French, Belgians and other people in Europe were not able to help.

With the declaration of war, Great Britain expected bombs to fall and mustard gas to fill the air. Mustard gas was used in WWI against our troops overseas in France and it actually burned their eyes and burned their bodies; it was a terrible death for them. Well, we were ready now for war or were we? No, it didn't happen that way. It started with a whimper and not a big bang. Thank goodness, for now us civilians had plenty of time to prepare for what was to be a seven year hiatus.

Everyone had to have a gas mask and mothers were to get their children used to them. They smelled of rubber and it was, horrible! The masks made us look like space aliens! People who worked at large stores would be 'sacked' or let go if they forgot their gas masks. Of course, being a three year old with a slightly younger sister, Janice, we were not really scared because we had Mummy and Daddy to protect us.

The government built brick shelters, but no one felt safe in them so everyone who had a garden built an Anderson shelter. The Anderson shelter became available in 1941, named after Sir John Anderson. My Dad, with the help of neighbors, dug a hole 6 feet deep and 7 feet wide, placed pieces of steel together to make a dome over this large hole with an entrance of steps to get inside and out, and mother rigged a piece of sacking to cover the front. Father, of course, then helped our neighbors build Anderson Shelters. Father also built bunk beds for us with straw pallets and my mother covered them with blanket material.

Somehow, today it reminds me of the concentration camps, although at that time we did not know of these things. No lights could shine out of the so-called doorways and air raid wardens came around to make sure no light was showing.

On top of the dome-shaped shelter, people planted grass seed or fruits and vegetables to help their family's food supply. My Grandfather Howells was the gardener in our family and he made me go outside with a shovel to scoop horse manure for his roses. No petrol was available so horses were back in vogue. Grandfather planted vegetables for us so we could have fresh vegetables instead of all the dried vegetables which were even used into the 1950's. And, yes, they were well washed before eating.

In the 1940's, we only had radio to give us the news. No television yet back then. We had the BBC (British Broadcasting Corporation) for all the news plus popular radio shows like "Worker's Playtime," a show broadcast from a factory where guns and tanks were being made, playing patriotic and popular sing along music to keep up the spirit of the workers. We had a gas cooker (gas stove) and Grandma Howells had a coal stove which heated the water in the back and facing the front was her oven. She used to put bricks in the oven and when she brought them out, she would cover them with towels and place them in our beds to warm them along with our pajamas.

Before the war began, Grandma Howells filled her food cellar with tinned peaches, salmon, pears, and tinned corned beef "Ready just in case," she said and people thought that Grandma was crazy doing this. Yes, crazy like a fox because on Sundays, during the war, my Grandma's was the most popular place to take High Tea. Somehow word got around that she always had a good spread.

We had no fresh eggs but mother actually purchased two for us girls as a treat, boiled them soft, placed them in egg cups with strips of bread that we called soldiers so we could dip them in the eggs but I hated them. I immediately hurried to the WC (the bathroom) to get rid of the awful taste. I don't think that I ever ate a fresh boiled egg for years to come. Much later my mother managed to get her hands on more eggs and preserved them in what was called Isinglass. Mother put apples and pears on pallets in the attic to keep them from going bad. No tropical fruit of course, because with our cold climate it was impossible to grow them and we did not have access to fruit from overseas during the war.

My baby sister, Ann, was born later when we moved to Whitkirk. When Janice and I found my Mum relaxing in the bathtub, we ran over to get my Aunt Alice Taylor. There were no doctors or midwives, just family to help. Aunt Alice screamed, "Get out of the bathtub or you'll drown the poor bugger!" After Mum gave birth, Ann was placed in her cot (crib) and mother and father had to get her a special gas mask that covered her entire body. Ann cried every time the gas mask was placed over her but she had to get use to it. To allow oxygen to get to her, it was necessary to pump it by hand like bellows. It would upset me and I started to cry as well. We were only allowed one bath a week. Imagine that with only very little

13

water and there just wasn't enough soap to be had with the small amount of coupons we received. By the way, I still have copies of identity cards and ration books.

All food was rationed and we needed food coupons. Even matches were sliced down the middle to make two. The butcher took money and coupons for meat for persons over six years of age and that was approximately only two ounces of meat per week. Fish was not rationed but it was scarce. Whale meat was available and oh, I do remember the whale oil. One night a week the fish and chips shop was open. We could smell it a mile away and they cooked with whale oil. We bought the fish and chips but never ate the whale meat although other people did and they even bought and ate it after the war in 1945, since rationing continued for quite a few more years. We were able to purchase corned beef in a tin from Argentina so Mother made corned beef fritters for us (recipe included).

Mum would purchase sausages (called bangers) from the butcher as part of our meat rations. They were made with very little pork and lots of bread filling so you had to prick them well with the fork before frying or baking them because if not, they would explode. We could now enjoy our favorite bangers and mash. Mash means mashed potatoes with onion gravy on top of the potatoes. I guess you would say we got more bang for the buck!

The people of London that were hit with real big bombs lost their homes and many lost their lives, many more people than we will ever know. Londoners used to go into tube stations underground every night regardless whether the bombs were coming or not, since you could never tell. This an underground city because no trains ran at night and it became a place to get a cup of tea and entertainment by buskers. Buskers were people who sang and entertained on roads above underground stations for a few pennies. People would 'bag' their own places (reserve unofficially) to stay for the night and heaven help anyone who stole their place.

When America got into the war, we were a broken nation. We needed all the help we could get and finally we got it because the Yanks were coming. British servicemen did not appreciate the fact, as the old expression goes, "These Yanks are over here, overpaid and oversexed." Of course, they courted the local girls with real nylon stockings, cigarettes, canned peaches, pineapple, and other foods we could not get. From the female point of view, they were demigods. Some girls married these Americans and would later travel on special boats to the United States. Most of them, called "war brides" would stay in the U.S. happily married forever, just visiting home to England now and again.

Unfortunately, some of the GI's, shall I say, pulled a fast one over on some of the local girls who were really uneducated. They were the only ones who fell for this. Remember this was in the 1940's and segregation was in effect in the U.S. Some girls were told their future husbands were night fliers to explain their black appearance. Of course, most of these girls never knew men of color and ended up getting married and going to the U.S. and in dire circumstances because they did not have a support group of their own race and were not accepted by either whites or blacks. This came into play later when my father became a politician and these war brides' parents came to him to find out how they could get their daughters back home to England.

By now, Winston Churchill and Clement Atlee acted together to have a combined government during the war years. As mentioned previously, the government would not let my father go to war. He had too much knowledge of electrical engineering and armaments and needed in Britain. Every day pamphlets arrived by post for housewives with tips on how to use their food coupons. People kept chickens, pigs, and rabbits

15

for their meat. Later after the war, we owned a pig because we had a restaurant and all the restaurant leftovers were put in the pig bin with all the other scraps, boiled to destroy bacteria and special pig meal was added, but as I said, this was after the war.

During the war, a lot of people had pigs and they kept chickens for their eggs. When the chickens could no longer lay eggs, they were put to use in the stew pot or in the roast pan. Chicken was considered a delicacy. People also raised rabbits strictly for the meat but sometimes it was hard for the younger ones, what they thought of as their pets, when it was time for slaughter. They used to have to do it discreetly but since they were rabbits and continually multiplying, the younger children were not aware that they were eating rabbit stew containing their pets.

One day when I was in primary school, the equivalent of elementary school, we had a raffle and the raffle was for a live rabbit or a jar of raspberry jam. Sugar during war time was in short supply so a jar of raspberry jam was quite a luxury. I won the raffle! I asked my mother's friend's son who was three years older to take the rabbit home for me and he said, "You must be barmy (crazy). I am a boy and far superior to you." So, I decided that I would take the jar of jam instead.

It so happened that I had to stay late after school that same day and school in England finished at four o'clock in the afternoon. During winter it got dark early which is when the bombing would begin but I still had to stay late to write 100 times "I must not talk in class." Finally, I finished and took my jar of jam and left to go home. It was already getting dark and suddenly the sirens went off. Well, I was in a field on my way home and couldn't do anything but lie flat, face down and place my hands over my ears so I would not be deaf if I survived. I hit the wet grass in the field and thank goodness I wasn't in cow manure, and one of the doodlebugs (bombs) dropped and the earth began to shake.

After the all clear siren was sounded, I got up with a bloody nose, completely covered in mud and to make matters even worse, my precious jar of jam was smashed. I picked up the smashed jar with the runny jam, put it all in my skirt, folded my skirt up to my waist and ran home to mother, crying my eyes out. Mother had a fit when she saw me as I looked much worse than I was because of all the dirt and my nose was bloody but I really wasn't hurt that bad. All I could do was drop the jar of jam all over the floor and cry. This broken jar of jam was more upsetting to me than the doodlebugs dropping in the field. This was my first culinary mishap.

After this incident, we were no longer kept late after school because it was winter and bombs were being dropped shortly after dark. These bombs were unmanned and made a buzzing sound and when the sound stopped, it meant they were dropping which is why I hit the ground like I did. Mother made scones (recipe included) but there was no raspberry jam.

Suddenly one day we noticed military personnel, big tanks and all other equipment, gun carriages loaded with guns were trundling down the streets of England heading for the coasts. Everyone came out and cheered them on because we knew something very big was going to happen in Europe and all we had to do now was pray and hope the news would be good. There were so many accounts of D Day with forces coming together. Americans, the British, even some free French and Polish people joined in helping advance toward Germany. The next news we heard was a radio broadcast by Richard Dimberly, a very famous news announcer and British war correspondent who had gone on many bombing missions over Germany. He was now at Belson Concentration Camp broadcasting for all of us to hear.

Very quietly, Richard Dimberly told listeners that it was the most horrible day of his life. It was hard to describe what he saw. There were 40,000 men, women and children in the camp who were German and at least half a dozen other nationalities. Thousands of them were Jewish and in the last few months alone, 30,000 prisoners had been killed or allowed to die. The next news heard was that Hitler was dead in his Berlin bunker. That, of course, was a celebration for us and we kids built a bonfire in the middle of the street. We even threw a few potatoes with their skins on into the fire to bake, calling them Jacket Potatoes. An effigy of Hitler was placed on the top of the fire to show that Hitler was dead. We chanted "Hitler is dead!" over and over again.

After Hitler's death, a news flash went around the country that Germany and Italy had surrendered. The announcement was officially given at 3 p.m. on May 2nd from the same room at 10 Downing Street that Chamberlain had announced the start of the war in 1939. Winston Churchill broadcast to the country and told us that Germany had signed an act of surrender of all German air, sea and land forces in Europe. Churchill also said that a very small period of rejoicing would be allowed but not to forget there is still Japan.

On May 7, everyone was running around trying to get pennants and flags. They rolled pianos out into the streets and had sing-a-longs. There were bonfires. Streets were lined with tables covered with food from the foods rations that housewives had kept hidden for this very special occasion or for an actual emergency. Once again church bells rang after having been silenced during the war. As darkness fell, ships had their flood lights on and ships in the harbor hooted a V sign and search lights cut "V's" in the sky representing Victory in Europe.

Londoners rushed to Buckingham Palace and stood outside while the King and Queen with the Royal Family and Winston Churchill came out on the balcony to wave to everyone. You see, even during the war, the Royal Family's children did not leave London seeking safety but a lot of children were sent north and were called refugees. Many of these children loved being there but others were very homesick.

Princess Elizabeth was driving motor vehicles and trucks for the military. One time, Buckingham Palace was hit with a bomb and a lot of damage was done. They were as much involved in the war and disaster as we all were. As we all know, in August atomic bombs were dropped on Hiroshima and Nagasaki and then on August 15, Japan surrendered. We celebrated once again. Eventually, service people were released from active duty, prisoners of war started to arrive home and the cost of war, nationwide, for Britain was 335,000 civilians non military. Just regular citizens including babies killed at the home front. That was nothing to cheer about. In fact, there were many, many tears at the end of the war.

The people of Britain decided that they wanted a change of government after the war years, so a general election was declared. Father was now to be a candidate for the Labour party and things would soon change for our family in a big way.

The following are war time recipes, and not to be taken seriously as today's recipes, but still fun to look back on when the world was at war, and I smashed my precious jar of jam in the bomb-dropping incident whilst going home.

CORNBEEF FRITTERS

This was part of our food ration, especially when fresh meat was not available. Served with tinned peas (fresh vegetables went to the troops) and if Mother had enough lard, she made homemade chips (french fries). I don't ever remember eating frozen fries until I came to the USA and even now at home, I make them fresh.

Open a tin of American Cornbeef and cut into thick slices. Flour them and set aside. Have a deep fat fryer ready at 350 degrees. Make a thick batter using Fish Batter mix from your grocery store or make your own with self-rising flour and beer thick enough to stick to the fritters. Tempura batter mix is lighter but can be used.

Place each slice of the beef into the batter and gradually lowered into the batter. Turn over the fritters when the bottom is golden brown. Remember the meat is precooked, so no need to leave it in the grease too long.

SCONES FOR AFTERNOON TEA WITH TODAY'S ADDITIONS

Sift together 2 cups Self-raising flour with 1 tsp. baking powder and pinch salt. Add 5 tbsps. Sugar (or less if rationed). Add ¼ pound margarine and rub into flour till like dried peas. Add 2/3 cup milk, knead together (will be sticky so use more flour if needed). Roll out until ½ inch thick. Use a biscuit cutter and place on greased tray a little apart to allow for rising. (After the war, we mixed ¼ cup raisins to the mix and egg wash, or brushed tops with milk). Reroll all the dough till used. Preheat oven to 425 degrees to allow for quick rising. Bake 10 to 12 minutes. Split and spread with margarine (wartime) or butter and jam.

Chapter

2 DAUGHTER OF A POLITICIAN

It was 1945 and the general elections were about to begin. My Father's Labour background was, as I stated in the first chapter, an electrical engineer. All the unions and the Co-Op Societies picked him to be their candidate for this life changing election for our family. Winston Churchill had performed well as a wartime Prime Minister but the people called for a change of government.

Clement Atlee, who would become the next Prime Minister, stayed at our home helping Father with his campaign. Mrs. Atlee always drove their car since back then it was unheard of to have a chauffeur or bodyguard. Father was elected as a member of parliament for Peterborough with a good majority of votes so our family moved to Peterborough in the county of Northamptonshire. Back in those days, a member of parliament earned a salary of six-hundred pounds a year, one-thousand dollars in US currency. With only this amount of money, he had to keep a home in Peterborough plus a place in London, so he shared a secretary with another MP (Member of Parliament, not military police) to help defray costs because he was out of pocket with the whole deal.

I must tell you that in recent years, politics have changed and in an article printed in the British Daily Mail on June 19, 2009, they called Clement Atlee, "One giant of a man, he was short and balding but stood for duty, decency and principle." What a contrast to this day's politicians. No wonder he was called one of the greatest prime ministers ever. I think that if he and my father were alive today, they would be disgusted with all the graft and greed with the current crop of government representatives in Great Britain, the U.S. and indeed all over the world.

Father's residence in London was at Mrs. Moffet's Boarding House. Quite a lot of MP's stayed there as she had an electric bell that was hooked up to the Houses of Parliament and it would ring when there would be a vote occurring. Then the members would race across the street to Parliament to vote.

We were very thankful that my grandparents gave us some of their food coupons to help when my parents entertained. Everybody in the election campaign would end up at our house after the meetings. This is the period when I took an interest in cooking which would last a lifetime, beginning at the early age of thirteen. It all started when I would make hors d'oeuvres like sardine pate on toast and battered fried spam bites on toothpicks (those fun recipes included). My sister Janice, eleven at the time, would write out the menus and place cards because mother attended the meetings as well. So, we were the chief cooks and bottle washers.

In my father's constituency lived the Duke and Duchess of Gloucester with their two children, Prince William and Prince Richard. I was picked up by their estate car and driven to play with the princes. I met the Duke and Duchess, gave a small curtsey and then the Princes were called out to meet me. I called them Prince only one time and then it was William, Richard and Pauline. I guess that I was deemed presentable in royal circles as I was a daughter of an M.P. We were to spend many times together playing and getting into mischief. Once we rode the ponies around the apple orchard and took too many green apples from the trees, called scrumping in England, and we got stomach ache. We went to the nursery for sandwiches made of honey which came from the estate's bee hives and fresh lemonade. I was to return many times. Prince William would in future be killed while flying his plane in the early 1970's, leaving Prince Richard to become the heir to the title of Duke when his father died.

I went with my father to different foreign embassy cocktail parties where he would confer with the ambassadors. I went sometimes when my mother would have other political duties to perform. As a teenager, I wore small heels, gloves, a small bag and a cute small cocktail hat. Quite grown up I thought.

Mother used to take me to the railway station in Peterborough, hand me over to the station master who would see that I was watched on the train when going to London to visit my father in Parliament. Father's secretary would pick me up in a taxi and drive to the Houses of Parliament, then up to the visitor's gallery where the public could watch the debates if they had a pass from their M.P. I would wave at my father but he would just nod his head as it would not be proper to wave back while in debate. It was normal for these debates to get quite rowdy with members banging on the floor to show their displeasure.

I would then go down and meet Father for lunch in the member's dining room with members of both political parties including the Prime Minister and of course Winston Churchill who was then head of the opposition party and as always smoking a cigar and drinking cognac. I did not realize how unusual this was. Didn't everyone sit down with cabinet members for lunch?

Father flew to Yugoslavia to meet with Marshal Tito for business reasons due to what was to be an inevitable takeover by the communists in the near future. After Father left Marshall Tito, he visited Czechoslovakia to meet with Jan Masaryk, where unpublished photographs were taken, one of which I have in my possession. Jan Masaryk confided in my father during that visit that he would be murdered, and so it was, with the communist party stating that the reason for his death was that he had committed suicide. Of course neither I nor my sister knew about this political intrigue but we were soon to be fully involved.

My father, mother, sister Janice and I left by propeller plane (no jets then) to Czechoslovakia on a government diplomatic mission.

We were met in Prague by communist agents, where we were driven to the Alkron Hotel where only foreigners were allowed to stay. It was so obvious that they were watching our every move and would take us to places they wished us to see. As I said, the hotel was for VIP guests, where the best food was available including foods that we had not had since before the war. We dined on goose, sweet dumplings, steaks, lamb and lobster plus other foods that the rest of the Czechoslovakian people were not able to get.

The Czechoslovakian people were without proper food or clothing. Janice and I were allowed to roam the streets though watched by communist bodyguards. Our parents were not worried as they knew the government would not let anything happen to us as we were Stanley Tiffany's daughters. This also left time for my father to plan his next steps and to find out what was really happening. People would come up to us and touch our Harris Tweed coats which were hand woven by Scottish weavers. Mother had saved her clothing coupons knowing that once I outgrew my coat, Janice would have it and then later Ann. We were not considered a threat to security as we were so young and naïve.

We had a female interpreter who took us on a river cruise and taught us a folk song that I remember to this day, but do not know how to write it down in their language. In later years, I sang this folk song quietly to Ivana Trump, wife of Donald Trump, when I was working in Palm Beach. Ivana cried and said to me, "How do you know this song?" I told her the story and she hugged me and thanked me for being a part of this adventure

24

even though I was too young at the time to realize its significance.

We were also taken to a factory in Bruno where glass was hand blown into magnificent glasses. My parents were presented with some lovely glass show pieces and a set of china, of which I still have a few pieces of the set, with some potent liqueurs and horrible cigarettes which they shipped to England for us.

One afternoon we were escorted to an open air communist meeting which included a bicycle race. Great Britain received a standing ovation when they entered the arena much to the chagrin of our escorts. Naturally, the home team got a standing ovation and the race concluded with a winner but I do not remember which team won. I was already getting a high temperature due to too much sun as we had light complexions. Later, when we returned home to England, the British team came to see my Father with important information from the Czechs.

Next morning, I was feeling much better. Our security agents came to escort us to another venue but my father instructed me to stay in bed and he told the men that, seeing as how sick I was, we would not be going out of the hotel. My red face told a story and my acting was superb, according to my father, and we were left alone though realizing that the hotel would be watched in case someone might visit us. As soon as the agents left and we watch them leave from our window, my father said to me, "Get dressed, we are going on a trip."

Father told us girls to stay quiet and not to say one word, as we had English accents and this fact would blow our cover. The maid came to our room after father had rung the bell, bringing breakfast rolls, butter, preserves and fruit, which we placed in mother's large bag, followed her down the hotel's corridors to a back entrance, which was checked out ahead of time for agents, then to a waiting old car.

We were to visit an English lady, who had taught English at the University of Prague, but was forbidden to teach anymore. Her husband was Czech and an airline pilot who had been stripped of his license for fear that he would try to hire or steal a plane to get his wife and young daughter out of the country. Their daughter was slightly younger than Janice and I but she used to come home from school with swastikas drawn on her back and lots of communist books and pamphlets for her to read about the wonderful communist party. Now I understood why mother had packed so many sweets from home and brought our breakfast foods that the maid had packed. These were for the little girl. Father and Mother conferred with the couple and Janice and I played with the girl in the house. We dared not be seen outdoors. Then we returned to the hotel from this hush hush trip.

Neither my sister nor I had any idea as to what our father was involved in. Later, we found out that he had helped many people escape from Czechoslovakia after the communists officially took over. You see, when communists take over a country, they also take over people's property and close their businesses for good. One of these families upon relocating to England was the Potter family. They had a business in Prague making toys so they started a factory in England. My sister Ann received a giant doll, as big as she was, that could walk with her when she held its hand. Janice and I received bears made from lamb's wool.

We left Czechoslovakia quickly as Father got word that the country was now officially being taken over by the Russians the next day. We were actually supposed to see Marshal Tito in Yugoslavia but under the circumstances it was better to head for England. We were deliberately detained at the airport in Prague to let us stew for quite a few hours, going through our luggage over and over again to show everyone that they were the bosses.

26

Upon returning to England, we picked up our little sister Ann, who had stayed with Aunt Alice and Uncle Vic, and gave her yet another small doll as a souvenir. This doll was in Czech costume to add to her collection from all over the world from father's missions but none quite like this last trip.

Since we were daughters of an M.P. we were not allowed to chew gum, couldn't ride our bicycles or wear shorts on Sundays but other than that we could come and go as we pleased. There was no such word as paparazzi but we did have a high wall surrounding the garden.

I remember our youngest sister Ann would go into the streets, unknown to us as to how she got out, but she would find the first Bobby (policeman), pull on his jacket and say, "Excuse me, sir, but I am lost and I'm Stanley Tiffany's little girl, so would you please take me home?" It was a ruse for her to get a sweet or two at the police station while they contacted my parents. Of course, we soon got wise to that trick.

We had a playground close to where we lived so Janice and I would ride our bikes to this place where there were swings and other games. We would play the game of rounder's which only girls played, as boys played cricket, soccer or rugby football. Rounder's is like American baseball but as I said this was a girl's game. I remember that I was standing too close to the batter and she hit me in the face with the bat. We left for home right away and by the time we arrived, my face was really swollen but no teeth were broken so Pauline would live to fight another day. At least there, there were no bombs exploding around me as did during the war that I talked about in the first chapter which just about ended my short life.

We certainly had a great life in Peterborough but soon the five years were up and another election was held to determine who was to be the M.P. for the next five years. My father lost the election by 250 votes due to changes in the county boundary lines. Now, home to Yorkshire with money from Janice, my savings accounts, money borrowed from my mother and father's sisters, we scraped enough money together to buy a café which was called Ann's Café in Wakefield with living accommodations above. It had belonged to my father's political agent's daughter, but she wished to immigrate to Australia. Since the café's name was also the name of our youngest sister, we did not change it and later there was to be a Pauline's Café in the same city.

My mother was a great home style cook and for the first time in his life, my father was at the fryer making fish and chips. I had never seen my father cook before. Don't think for a moment that just because he was no longer a member of parliament that he was out of the political game. Oh, no sir!!! The Right Honorable Arthur Creech Jones wanted my father to take a 'safe seat' (safe meaning a sure bet) but due to a bad fall that happened at a political rally where a British Earl with one hellish temper clobbered poor Father on the head with his cane, sent Father "Down for a Burton." Unfortunately, from that day on he had a bad back, even though the Manor House Hospital, where the top people go for surgery, sent a team to Peterborough for Father's operation, but he did not fully recover. Father refused Arthur's offer but was instead voted head of the Council. Later he received the CBE (Commander of the British Empire) from the Queen.

28

FRIED SPAM BITES ON TOOTHPICKS WITH MUSTARD

Same recipe as the cornbeef batter. Cut the Spam (specialized processed American meats) into bite-sized cubes. Dredge in flour, then dip in same batter as the Cornbeef Fritters and drop into 350 degrees fat to brown. Drain on towels and place on toothpicks, serve with hot mustard.

SARDINE PATE ON TOAST

Use sardines in oil, drain out oil. Then mash together. Spread on small squares of toast. Sprig of parsley on top.

Remember, these recipes are not for today's taste, but to show you what we did to get through the war and just after the war, as rations were still in force and things were not back to prewar years for quite a few more years.

Chapter

3 CAFE LIVING & THE MALE COLLEGE

Now here we were living above Ann's Café. We lived in one room that was our personal dining room and it acted as our front room with an area cordoned off with a curtain for privacy, where we could take a sponge bath as we had no regular bath. Every week I would go to the public baths, a combination of cubicle bathrooms where the lady in charge would draw your bath water. I always took my own towels and flannels (wash cloths). Mother had her washing machine in the potato room, so called because we had potato sacks stashed there with the latest high tech potato peeler for the pounds of chips and mashed spuds that we prepared every day.

This was no "Daughter of a Politician" lifestyle anymore that's for sure. Down the hallway was the W.C. to be used by us and the customers. Our hanging clothes in a wardrobe on the landing gradually permeated with the smell of fish and chip grease. Therefore, we usually put our clothes on the outside clothes line to dispel the smells before we went anywhere, as we were embarrassed in case anyone could detect the grease. We had two bedrooms on the top floor, one for our parents and one for three girls. My sister Janice had her own bed since she did not wish to have Ann sleep with her as she said that Ann kicked her all night and would grind her teeth.

I worked in the café evenings and weekends. At that time, Janice was not at all interested in waitress or cook work so I helped. I even opened up on Sunday mornings so my parents could sleep in. I would park our bicycles outside the front entrance, trying to entice bicyclists to stop for a bite to eat. As they say advertising pays and even then I seemed to have the knowhow to get people to come by and spend their money.

After high school was finished for my sister and me, Janice went to Sheffield to get her teaching degree and lived away from home. I stayed living with my family and was offered a place at the Hotel and Catering College in Huddersfield. Wonders never cease, as I was a girl in a man's world already. There were no other females accepted, education back then was free in England so here was the question. Why send a female into a man's domain when she would get married after using taxpayer money and stop a male candidate from the position?

My family was already in the trade so they took a chance and gave me a place in this all male Huddersfield Hotel and Catering College program. I took the double decker bus every week day to Huddersfield, sitting on the top tier where I could smoke my fag (cigarette) clinging to my hot water bottle with fur lined boots on to keep me warm. There was no heating on the bus and we were traveling over the Pennine Range, very high, windy and foggy, stopping along the way to pick up passengers.

Before I left college to go home in the evenings, I would once again fill my hot water bottle and prayed that we would get through the heavy, damp fog before night set in. Yes, it was quite a journey and I did it every weekday. Sometimes in autumn and winter there was so much fog that passengers would actually lead the bus with a flashlight to get us home safe, no backup buses to rescue us. Who would possibly come and get us in this black icy fog?

My father bought another café, as business was good, serving the same plain Yorkshire food to the working man whose main meal of the day was lunch. We served three courses; soup, main course and pudding (dessert) for two shillings and six pence. This new café was called Pauline's, after me, and we had two floors of dining rooms which were forever filled at lunch time and especially busy all day until closing during market days. Market days were Wednesday and Saturday with much bustling around down below in the market place, stalls full of fruits, vegetables, meats and fish, plus china and clothing at very cheap prices. Mother's hot rice pudding was a favorite at both cafes (recipe included). I worked there every weekend after my college week was over until closing at 8:00 p.m. Then my best friend Margaret and I would go dancing at the Embassy Ballroom where we met friends Terry, Danny and Sheila. Our feet were killing us after running up and downstairs serving customers but we had to go dancing and then walked home without wearing our shoes, even if it was freezing outside.

In college, our chef instructor Monsieur Surtees demonstrated a four course meal for us which we then prepared the same meal in small individual kitchens next day. After the dishes were critiqued by Chef Surtees, the food was sent to the waiter's instruction dining room for our fellow students who were doing their waiter training. They served this food to many teachers from all parts of the college and there was always a waiting list for "the best food in town." In the kitchens, the male students would wear the typical chef uniform while I had to wear a cook's dress, as pants were not proper for ladies.

Our turn came to be waiters in training, learning full French silver service plus the art of wine and cocktail service. The men wore black pants, white shirts, bow ties and jackets with long crisp, starched aprons. I wore a black, long sleeve dress with a heavy starched white collar which rubbed my neck raw, white celluloid cuffs to protect my arms from the searing heat of the silver platters, and a heavy starched crisp white apron. Mr. Wentworth, our waiting instructor would have me bend over, as if I was serving, so that he could make sure that my slip did not show and that my black stocking seams were straight. So damned humiliating but what could I do? There were African princes taking our courses to enable them, on their return home, to explain to their people how to treat and entertain foreign guests. I was very surprised when they came the first day wearing their tribal dress.

The same people traveled everyday on the bus I took to get home but I was the only student. Friday was the day we all looked forward to because people were going home for the weekend, and here was Pauline with boxes filled with fresh pastries that I had made and also purchased from other students who preferred shillings for their beer after pastry class, so everyone loved Fridays. I had to make sure I had some of my own pastries for my family and our restaurant staff, waiting patiently for me. I was definitely the most popular member on the bus.

During summer vacation we had to work in a hotel, club or fine dining restaurant approved by the college, so even if we had six weeks off, we actually had just one week and the rest was used for more hands on training. I picked the Old Swan Hotel in Harrogate. One of my friends, Margo, worked there as head receptionist and we remain friends to this day having a long continued friendship. I lived in the hotel for the duration in horrible staff quarters that were damp and miserable. This hotel had quite a history as it was an old coaching inn. They had an employee outside in breeches and top hat blowing a hunting horn when expensive coaches with Americans would drive up to spend a few days as this town was quite spectacular. The hotel was used for the back drop of a movie called "Agatha" showing the life of Agatha Christie during her so called 'disappearing act' at this hotel. The movie featured Dustin Hoffman as an American journalist and Vanessa Redgrave starred as Agatha. Different scenes were shot inside the hotel and parts of the town. I still have the movie.

The town of Harrogate is so beautiful with lots of open, manicured public parks. The Stray is where nannies would walk their charge in prestigious prams and a bridle path for horses ridden by gentry. This land is public domain and can never be

33

changed, thank goodness. The shops and antique stores were very upscale, catering to wealthy people who made this town their home. A century ago, there were Roman baths where people would bathe in the medicinal waters but has since turned into a museum where you could take a glass of this horrible acidic tasting water.

I much preferred to go to Betty's Café for afternoon tea and where the waitresses wore black dresses with little frilly tea aprons. Everything was served on silver with foods consisting of hot crumpets, scones with clotted cream and jam, tiny finger sandwiches (recipes included) and a sweet trolley was wheeled around with fabulous desserts. I did not realize it then but I would put this idea of a sweet trolley into use at our future family hotels. And then much later, I had the rolling dessert cart as my special signature for the top rated restaurant Bon Appétit, which was where I was featured in the Kiplinger Changing Times Magazine (centerfold no less) showing me pushing the dessert cart in one of many photographs, along with a five page article telling its readers about how to run a good restaurant.

A lot of older ladies who lived in the hotel as permanent guests would dress for dinner, coming down from their rooms or suites wearing diamonds and pearls. These ladies would have their beverage of choice hidden under their mink stoles, then they would place their bottles under their table so they would not have to pay a bar fee for their drinks. The staff pretended not to notice but our eyes were much younger than theirs.

I would stop by the reception desk to visit with my friend Margo, our eyes pinned to the door just in case Mr. Jeffrey Wright M.H.C.I. (Great Britain) would appear. He was the general manager and had the designation that I wished somehow to achieve. Yes, I did later achieve the designation from The City and Guilds of London. Another plus was that Margo's future husband was to achieve the same designation after seeing me come back from college every day, telling my tales and eating my goodies. Terry was a customer, boyfriend and best of all like a brother to me.

Now back to college for our final year, having become much wiser for all our experiences during vacation. Of course, we had learned quite a lot and shared stories with our classmates and instructors. My final exams were at the end of the year. Chef Surtees took four students at a time into one of the small kitchens where we used to cook for four persons. He and Chef Judges were to be our examiners. Chef Surtees would stand outside with smelling salts and brandy in case they were needed and they were. All wasted food was weighed by these judges to see how frugal we were. Since my last name was Tiffany, toward the end of the alphabet list, I was to see my friends coming out of this five hour grueling exam looking absolutely shattered.

This exam was no piece of cake as I had to prove my ability as a female. Remember, there were only males in prestigious hotel kitchens and even pot washers were males so, as they say, I was there "where no female in her right mind" had been before. Getting to college on time for my exams was quite a hassle because I had to be there early, so I begged my next-door neighbor to take me on his motorbike. There I was in my billowing whites on the back of a bike going to take my five hour cooking exam, being escorted to the W.C. by a female staff member who also watched me at the five minute break time. Chef Surtees came with a cup of Yorkshire tea, winking at me as he set the cup down, and squeezed my hand to give me some badly needed confidence.

My waiter training exam was quite something else. In the kitchen they made an omelet allowing it to get stuck to the bottom of the silver platter that I was serving it from. There I was, feeling ill with a high temperature that day, trying my best to get it free and serve it. Well, I did, with a sigh of relief that even the customers heard as they smiled at me and gave me the

35

thumbs up. Many more problems were placed before me to solve, for instance when I first entered the dining room I noticed that my table was wobbly so I moved it around to correct it. No, friends, and I hope I can now call you a friend; it was not permissible to place a matchbook under the legs.

I passed all my exams with flying colors but the jobs available for me were more in the management of dining rooms. These positions were not college material at all but I was in no rush as my parents insisted that I took a position worthy of my college background. Eventually I was offered the position of assistant manager of a first class rated and largest hotel in Leicester.

Now the point of getting my degree was to procure a management position in a fine hotel. My father had visualized our family somehow purchasing a hotel in the future after I gained actual hotel experience, which I did, but he had not taken into consideration something called LOVE.

ASSORTED AFTERNOON TEA SANDWICHES

Use extra thin Pepperidge Farm bread. Take a few slices of both kinds of bread, ready to start. Cut off the crusts (see how easy it gives a clean cut when it is frozen) and cover with a towel to keep it moist.

Make an egg salad but make sure the celery is super dry. I use a little sweet relish, the egg and a little dry celery plus a pinch of chopped parsley. Then just a little mayonnaise to moisten, salt sparingly and pepper. Slice cucumbers after peeling thin and cover with a little salt (to bring out the water), then rinse and dry really well.

Slice very thin, a cooked cold chicken breast. Set aside. Thin slices of smoke salmon (not lox) ready, plus a few slices of seedless lemon and parsley for garnish. Now you are ready to make an afternoon tea "fit for a Queen." Take a few slices of white bread and butter, then lay a thin layer of cucumber slices, then place on the other white bread slice. Gently press down. Cut into triangles and place on a covered tray.

Take a few slices of wheat bread, butter very lightly and lay on thin slices of smoked salmon (squeeze a little lemon on top), then place other wheat bread on top. Do not salt, as salmon is salty.

The egg salad should be thinly placed on the white bread with a few watercress leaves on top, then a wholewheat bread slice on top. Press down lightly. Keep the tray with the largest part on the bottom, then stack up the rest of the sandwiches, leaning up against the first with parsley to accent the platter. Now you have a nice selection of Afternoon Sandwiches for tea time to be accompanied by pastries and tarts.

MOTHER'S RICE PUDDING

When we first opened Ann's Café, my Mother used this recipe for the Rice Pudding as well as all the steamed Jam Roly Poly, College Pudding and Spotted Dick, but to the American palate, most were alien except the Rice Pudding – so here is the recipe for Rice Pudding from Ann's Café and Pauline's Café. This pudding is served hot, not cold (as in the USA). Often we place a dollop of jam on top, before serving.

Wash ½ cup short grain rice (not long grain). Butter a one quart dish, and place the washed rice in the bottom of the dish. In a saucepan, heat 3 cups whole milk, pinc salt, ½ cup sugar and ¼ teaspoon vanilla essence. Never use artificial extract. Simmer to melt sugar and cover rice. Place a few pieces of butter on top and a sprinkle of nutmeg. Place in the oven and cook at 275 degrees, slow cooking for 2 ½ hours, but do stir after a few hours – then add more butter pats and nutmeg on top. Cook for 2 ½ hours.

I must bring back a minute in time, from the war years, when my Grandmother used to bake my Grandfather a rice pudding in her coal oven and told me that my Grandfather loved the crust on top but let me have this crusty top as a treat.

Chapter

4   THE GRAND HOTEL, LEICESTER

After college, I was recruited by the general manager of the famous Grand Hotel in Leicester, a beautiful Victorian hotel and the largest in the city, a venue for banquets, balls, weddings and other extravagant affairs. I was now the assistant manager, the only female in management so it was a lonely life at first because I was not able to make friends with other employees due to my position as a boss.

I occupied a small room with a bed, wardrobe and small bedside table which had a small cupboard underneath to hold a guzunder (goes under) which is a chamber pot used during the night to stop trips to a cold bathroom. I shared a bathroom located down a long hall with other females and I would get up at 5:00 a.m. to be first to bathe (no showers back then) and join the head housekeeper in her sitting room where I enjoyed all my meals. Our meals were served by commis (learner) waiters who were shaking in their boots as we had to report on their service to the head waiter in the main dining room. Somehow it reminded me of my college days.

My duties varied each day, some days I would be in housekeeping checking the rooms after the guests left and I wore a belt that held keys so that I could enter any room in the hotel. When I did room checks, I held the keys close to my body so they would not jingle and alert the maids that I was coming. I wore white cotton gloves to check for dust and I was also checking to see if the maids were working, sitting on the beds or watching television. There was the time that an American band (entertaining at the local concert hall), managed to con some of our maids into having sex with them in their rooms. Some of these girls were recently from Barbados and had no idea that this was wrong, having only been in this country for a short time.

Unfortunately they were fired and sent back to their homes and the band was asked to leave the hotel.

Liberace, a famous American entertainer and pianist, stayed at the hotel and had a suite of six rooms. I was responsible for obtaining two grand pianos for him to practice on and had them delivered and tuned and placed in two of his sitting rooms. Liberace had so many clothes for his stage performances that they filled one of the large bedrooms where we had placed extra wardrobes to handle all the sable, mink and other coats plus very ornate costumes for his act. He traveled with a large staff and they also stayed in the hotel.

I was making ten pounds a week plus, as we say, room and board which was quite a tidy sum in those days. I was able to purchase a radio and record player and records of my favorite artists. I used to take trips quite a long time ago with my friends to see these artists perform. My favorite was Johnnie Ray who came to stay at the Grand for a few days. I made a special check of his room to make sure that the food and drinks that his manager had pre-ordered were in his suite. He was as handsome as I remember but I was gob smacked when I saw his boyfriend with him. I never had a crush on any star again.

Downstairs under an archway next to the hotel was the hotel beauty shop. As an employee of the Hotel, I paid less than the guests so I always looked presentable even if my feet were swollen and my body tired. The beauty shop was where I later literally ran into my future husband, James.

Leicester was a main center for the shoe trade so on weekdays the hotel was filled with salesman and the suites booked by factory owners and out of country buyers for big overseas contracts. I met one of the largest shoe company owners in the country and his name was Sidney. His company name was on at least one store in a small town and three or more stores in the cities. Sidney took a fancy to me and dated me in royal style, having his Rolls Royce with driver pick me up to go on trips, away from the city, to fine country restaurants for dinner and a show. Sidney was a real gentleman and even my grandmother was stoked with him but he was not the one for me. After all, I had just started my journey into the hotel business and had a lot to learn.

I was able to take the train home to visit my family and my dear Aunt Flo who was in hospice dying of cancer. Later, I would understand what hospice stood for when I catered a party which introduced hospice into the U.S. I would take the late train back to Leicester on Sunday night ready for work the next day, or my family would come to see me and take me out for dinner before going back to Yorkshire.

The head chef is in charge of the kitchen and responsible for what occurs in his exclusive domain. There was a brass strip running across the kitchen floor showing that this was off limits, even to the general manager who rarely stepped onto this hallowed ground even though he was a male. The chef was the ruler of this part of the hotel and heaven help anyone who crossed this brass strip, unless they were invited.

A new gourmet style buffet bar was built downstairs with copper counters and small copper plated tables that required polishing every day. The food was prepared in the main kitchen upstairs and brought down by cart in one of the service lifts. The head chef had control as to what foods were to be used in this bar mainly serving favorite foods such as planked Scottish smoked salmon and York ham, carved in front of the customers along with cold roast sirloin of beef. Also served were Melton Mobray pies, pork pies, potted shrimp served with thin toast (recipe included) and fresh salads including Russian salad and a new addition called American potato salad, British pickles, relishes and fresh bread rolls from our own bakery department. Of course, desserts included apple pie, lots of delicious clotted cream from Devon to smother all the other pastries sent from the pastry department, plus lots of good cheeses and no knowledge of calories or cholesterol back then. Phil was the name of our buffet bar chef and he had a female partner to serve and assist him.

No sooner had this venue opened to much publicity; Chef Phil was found drunk and unable to work. As it happened that I was the only person capable of running this project, as quick as I could, I changed into appropriate attire to work behind the bar, carving and serving customers. I figured this was just until the head chef could find a replacement but I was so very wrong, as apparently this chef realized that here was this female that could run rings around any of his brigade and my relationship with him was changed. After this, he showed respect for me that he had never dreamed would ever happen in his male only kitchen. I could go into the kitchen, place my orders, and also ask for special items such as brown Windsor soup (recipe included) and shepherds' pie that I knew I could sell. The buffet bar became busy and business was better than ever. Chef became a good friend and many evenings I would visit him and his wife at their home where we enjoyed champagne and beluga triple 0 caviar. Chef would send me back to the hotel in a taxi, saying it was not good for a young lady to walk alone in the evenings as there were so many drunken American solders walking around with ladies of ill repute.

The hotel hired a new head accountant and hurrah this person was female. She and I soon became good friends, as she was considered executive staff. She moved into the hotel and we moved into a larger room together. It had two large beds and a dining table with chairs so we could bring our meals upstairs. We even had an electric fireplace so we were much warmer than before. We would go to the cinema, a few local watering holes and the dance halls to enjoy ourselves. We even went on dates to local attractions and out into the country if our dates had a car. We shopped till we dropped enjoying the money that we earned.

On many weekends when I was free, we took off for London on the train from Leicester then take the boat train to Paris for the weekend, booking a sleeper so that we could regenerate our bodies from the long week to be awakened in Paris to fresh croissants and preserves with our beverages. I never liked coffee and have avoided it all my life. What a life with all the shops and restaurants in Paris to be enjoyed. Before we knew it, we were back on the train to work arriving early on Monday morning rejuvenated. I kept a diary during this period and noted that a lot of my pages were full of working over twelve hours every day and there I was still stuck in the buffet bar during the day, in banquets until early hours of the morning and getting very little sleep. I took sick from fatigue but the hotel doctor soon had me back to work.

I was on to my way to the beauty shop one day when I fell slap bang into James, my future, first husband. He laddered my fifteen derriere nylon stockings but arrived the next day at the reception desk with replacements. He was a charmer. He was a Yank and accordingly looked down upon by British men. I could not say that I blamed them because of the way that a lot of Yanks had generally misbehaved. I fell hook, line, and sinker for James. His friends called me to say that he was a liar and married to an Air Force lieutenant but he said that he was divorced. I never told my family about this first marriage as already my father was unhappy and pulled enough strings to send him back to the U.S. but James kept returning by thumbing a lift, shall we say, the lift being by military plane. Eventually, my family relented and we became engaged. I wrote to his mother and sister–in–law in the U.S. James was sent to an Air Force base in Georgia.

Christmas was coming and I was to join my family for a vacation at Blackpool, a popular seaside resort, and I had my bags packed. My roommate had already left to visit her family when there was a knock on the door. Upon opening the door, I saw my boss who wished me a Merry Christmas but continued

43

by telling me that he loved me and wished that I would forget James and hurry back to him. Well, you could have knocked me down with a feather. I told him no way so he threw me onto my bed and we struggled as he tried to rape me. Thankfully, I was too quick for him and he was so heavy that his movements were not fast enough. I ran to the door, opened it, and demanded that he get out or I would scream bloody murder and bring the entire hotel staff to my aid. He left very quickly. He did not want to be found in the female rooms where no males were allowed, including the manager. I quickly got my clothes and personal belongings together and called a taxi to take me to the train station, using the back entrance. I was nineteen, in shock and so traumatized having never been through this sort of carrying on. I was in no mood to explain to anyone what had just happened.

I arrived at the private hotel in Blackpool well ahead of my family who were quite surprised to see me so early. I managed to get my mother and father alone and told them what had just happened to me and asked them to keep quiet, since my entire family including grandmother, aunts, uncles and my two sisters were there to have a good time. They promised they would say nothing but Father called my old boss. I was not told what was said but I am sure enough was said for him to worry about his job and marriage. He apparently gave notice and left quickly, hoping to take another job elsewhere. I wonder what excuse he gave his wife for their quick moonlight flit before too many people, including my friend Doreen, got wind of what had occurred. Doreen called and came to visit me at home, where I told her the full story. She had taken a new job elsewhere with better pay.

Now I was spending my time getting ready for my big adventure, to go with my mother to the U.S. to get married and hope to live in peace forever. Well, the next chapter will tell you about the world I was about to see when I arrived to get married and was confronted with sheer craziness and guns.

BROWN WINDSOR SOUP

Do not compare this hearty soup with the tinned or powdered variation that reminds me of war time fare. Great nourishing soup; a meal in itself to be served with rolls and butter.

2 ounces butter melted in a good heavy saucepan
Add 1 pound lean stew beef (cut into small pieces)
3 onions finally chopped and 2 carrots also chopped
Sauté till all is brown.

Add 4 tbsps. flour and stir to cook flour and then add 10 cups of beef stock (use the grocery store beef stock).

Add ½ tsp. thyme, ½ tsp. tarragon, 1 bayleaf, salt and pepper. Before we get any further, I must stress that dry herbs and spices have a very small life, unless (like me), you refrigerate them. Please keep this in mind.

Cover and simmer 2 hours. Season to taste with salt & pepper. Now blend the soup or process. Reheat and add 1 cup Madeira wine. Season to taste.

POTTED SHRIMP

One of the most requested appetizers to start a meal or as a bar snack.

Defrost, drain and dry on paper towels 1 pound tiny cooked shrimp. Place half in the blender just on and off for a minute to rough chop. Take from blender.

Have a frying pan ready on low heat, melt ¼ pound unsalted butter. Add ½ tsp. mace, 1 bayleaf, and if available at your store, a pinch of shrimp base. Stir and salt & pepper to taste. If no shrimp base, then grind more shrimp in the blender until mush and add to pan with the rest of the shrimp. Toss to mix and get the flavor. Then place into small ramakins (tiny bowls to hold approximately ½ cup, well packed). Now cover with clarified butter to give it a long shelf life. Serve with thin-cut whole grain bread triangles. Place a piece of lemon for garnish and to taste.

Clarified Butter:
Very slowly melt unsalted butter (it will have milk solids on the base). Skim the butter fat from the top and strain this clear yellow liquid into a container. This method is used for many especially fine French dishes. Discard the milk from the pan.

Chapter

5 WEDDINGS & THE GUN DISASTER

My parents threw a huge party at Pauline's Café before I left for the U.S. to get married. The Mayor and Mayoress of our hometown attended, wearing their ceremonial robes and chains of office, and all the staff of Ann's Café and Pauline's Café plus other family and friends were there. An open bar with elegant but substantial finger food was catered by our local baker and caterer. My father arranged for a professional film company to document the occasion and I still enjoy looking at this video. Music was hired to entertain the guests but, believe me, my family proved to be "sing along experts" and it was not long before the Mayors' party took off their chains of office which my father placed in the safe so they could let their hair down.

My aunt Alice Taylor was a fabulous baker and made a three-tier heavy fruit cake, soaked in brandy for over six months, then covered it with marzipan and royal icing which is hard and keeps the cake for years. My father's cousin's daughter kept her top cake for eight years for her baby's christening. We used the top tier for this party, then the other two tiers were placed in padded boxes made by our local undertaker, from wood used for his coffin business, with ornate handles on the tops for us to hand carry to the U.S. aboard the boat, then to carry to St. Augustine, Florida.

My mother was to come with me on the ship with all my wedding gifts and instruction from Father to bring me back home if anything was out of place. We left on the train with my grandmother who would accompany my mother and me to the boat. Many of our family and friends were at the train station to see us off and for the first time in my life, my father was crying as he held onto my hand as the train began to depart. Off we went on our long voyage to New York.

When the boat docked in New York, my future U.S. family was there to greet us and they had this big red Dodge with large fin like fenders. I had never seen such a big car. Even a Rolls Royce, Bentley or a Jaguar, which was what my father owned and was his favorite car, looked small compared to the Dodge. We drove through parts of New York City before driving through a tunnel headed for their home in New Jersey. The traffic was going so fast that it left me breathless, even London was slow compared to this speed. Our luggage was sent by truck on its way to St. Augustine, though I did not know at the time the meaning of the word truck as we called it a lorry, except for the wedding cakes which mother and I hand carried.

When we arrived at their house, we ate southern fried chicken which Mother and I had never tasted before since in Britain, it was considered bad manners to use your fingers. We always used a knife and fork like the rest of Europe but I enjoyed this new experience, along with my first taste of creamed corn. I noticed that a lot of teenagers were hanging around the house, probably curious about this English girl with a strange accent and which I still proudly have to this day. Most of these teens were in college which almost anyone can attend after high school in the U.S., whereas in Britain, a lot of students compete for a few places, being more conservative as to who attends and my mother was very proud that two of her daughters were in college. In the U.S., banks give loans and students can receive college scholarships to help pay for higher education but only what was called top students could attend college in Great Britain, and it was free. There were also special schools that taught different trades or vocations for those not going to college.

The next day we flew on a plane to Jacksonville, Florida, an entirely different type of living in what is called the sunshine state. My future husband and his mother were there to greet us and we motored to St. Augustine in another huge car, this time a Lincoln with air conditioning which we never had in our cars at home. At home, we would drive with the windows down if we were lucky enough to see the sun. On arriving at their house, we were greeted by the maid, who had prepared a meal for us.

When Mother and I were about to retire for the night, I said to my future husband, "Please knock us up in the morning," and I thought his mother was going to have a fit as you see this expression in our country means to knock on the door to wake us up. That was all it meant but at that time it meant something entirely different in the U.S.

There were many parties to introduce me to the friends and family down south as they say. I went to a wonderful beach where James drove on firm sand, showed me around and introduced me to a drive-in restaurant where I ordered fried chicken and salad with French dressing which to my amazement was orange and came out of a bottle. French dressing to me was vinaigrette, so I was learning new things all the time. My mother went out with James' mother to see the oldest city in the U.S.; so quaint with a much slower pace than New York but so hot, as it was August and we were not used to so much heat and high humidity.

Unfortunately, we did not realize and maybe my future husband did not know all the facts, but his mother was an alcoholic and a drug addict with heavy mood swings and even threatened us with a gun. Apparently she kept this gun for protection from what she called bad niggers. We did not have guns in England for the masses; even the police did not have guns, so both Mother and I were petrified. The reason we were being threatened with a gun had nothing to do with bad niggers, as she called people of color. It was because cousin Rosa, who was the matriarch of the family and owned the Bennett Hotel opposite the Castillo de San Marcos, was a devout Catholic and James' mother wanted us to be married in the Cathedral and I had to swear that any children would be brought up Catholic. Strange thing was that James, his mother, nor any other

49

members of the family were Catholic, so quite frankly, I did not understand his mother being so upset. But, she was because she saw herself as heir to cousin Rosa's estate and said that I should marry Catholic. I refused as I was from the Church of England and my parents would not approve.

I was so scared and had never seen a real gun before. She must have had a sudden sense of reality and took the gun into her bedroom. We learned more when James' brother arrived for the wedding, that apparently their mother used her third husband's Demerol which had been prescribed when he was in pain and dying. Sadly, both of her sons were never close to her and left home early after having been at five different schools (all military schools), so they had a pretty lousy home life. James never shared any of this with me.

We decided to go on with the wedding but to this day I remember very little about it as I was in shock. I do remember that I made all the foods for the reception and took a total of four showers that day. Mother took movies with Father's camera to take back .home. I swore my mother to secrecy and told her not to say a word to my family. I must admit she was like putty in my hands, and after the wedding, Mother went with James' uncle to his house to be safe while we had a three-day honeymoon in Daytona Beach with my new brother and sister-in-law. That was an unusual honeymoon to say the least but I had never been on a honeymoon before and in a strange new country, so I was not sure as to what was normal.

Looking at James' mother, you would never think she could be crazy. She dressed well, had southern charm, always wore gloves and had good manners except when she was cuckoo. I was instructed to always stay on the sidewalk when a colored person passed me, making them step out into the street and not to have any conversation with them except to give them instruction when they were working for me. I had no idea about discrimination because the only colored people that I had ever

50

seen were the African princes when I attended college and they had been treated just the same as the rest of us students.

It was obvious that I could not stay in this city, so Mother and I went with my sister-in-law and brother-in-law on the train back to their home in New Jersey. I had to leave most of my wedding gifts in their mother's garage as once again we were threatened so we had to high tail it out of there fast. My husband was still in the military and had to report back to his base. I took my mother to the boat with both of us crying our eyes out. I was worried that maybe I would never see her again but little did we both know that it would be sooner than we could have imagined.

Now living without my mother and new husband, I had to get a job so I went to an employment agency. Upon seeing my qualifications, they offered me a job as an executive housekeeper at the Waldorf Astoria in New York but I was now married and could not see myself alone in this busy city and away from the only people that I knew in this new world, so I did not accept the offer.

Instead, I took a job waiting tables in a restaurant that was called a diner. I had never been in a diner before or had even heard of such a place but I definitely knew how to wait tables, or at least I thought I did, but this was a different country and service was much more casual. I had an English accent which was a novelty and well received by the regular customers except one day I was waiting on three customers at the counter when one of them told me to go back home where I belonged. They were of Irish descent dating back many decades but still had a hatred for the British which I could not fathom. I had many friends in Ireland and loved the countryside as well as the people. The regular customers practically threw these men out of the diner.

My husband returned to civilian life but jobs were scarce and he had no specialized civilian qualifications. He got a job as a milkman but when it came to making up the bills for the customers he was hopeless, so I helped him. I realized that his education had not been the best, probably due to his mother changing his school so many times. I was still working at the diner when I found out that I was pregnant and we had no military help.

While James had still been in the military, his brother tried to seduce me and on telling my husband about it, James never said a word to his brother but we did move to his uncle's house, on his deceased fathers' side. This was Uncle Charlie and Aunt Dot. They were a wonderful family and I was made to feel so welcome. I was still working but with morning sickness and no doctor to help me, so I was not feeling the best. I knew that I needed to do something to get help because we had no health insurance, which was free in Europe, and James could not get a job due to a recession (which is kind of true but not the real reason). So my father arranged for the purchase of tickets home as we still had a few wedding gifts that we had managed to recover from James' mother's garage during our hasty retreat.

As soon as my family got the news of my homecoming, they set about hurriedly preparing the top floor over the restaurant dining rooms, into a fabulous apartment with furniture that was needed, a nursery for the baby and a small kitchen so that I could prepare meals if the restaurant was closed. The cot (crib) was mine and my sister's when we were born and my extended family painted, wallpapered and hung drapes to make it a great home. My parents wanted to buy the baby a top of the line pram but I insisted that I was going to put it on the never-never as we called credit. So, I purchased a Wilson pram, in white with a royal crown derby rose painted on each side of the body. This pram was to stay in our family and wheel all of my children for many years to come. I had a photograph taken after my second child was born which showed both children out for a walk in their pram.

I stayed active and even though I was very slim; my Father insisted that I drink a bottle of Guinness each day for nourishment and breast milk production as most women breastfed their little ones and rarely used bottle feedings unless absolutely necessary. I worked in the kitchen until the last month of pregnancy, then taking care of the cash as no credit cards or checks were used back then, so it was a cushy job and kept me in touch with the customers. A lot of them were my friends from before my marriage.

James was supposed to be learning the business and was to stoke up the Aga cooker which that was our main cooking range with the coke brought up from the cellar. He hated to get out of bed so I ended up going into the cellar with the buckets to do his job. I did not want my father to know that he was not pulling his weight and thankfully it did not cause any damage to me or the baby. My husband became a very good customer at the pub next to the restaurant and I saw him involved in friendly conversation with two women in the market place. He was now the oddity with an American accent and I was to see this sort of thing happening several times but I kept my mouth shut as I didn't think it would do any good to say anything. Divorce at that time was more or less unheard of and I dreaded to hear my father say, "I told you so."

Heaven help us. James' mother arrived from the U.S and my family welcomed her as we knew that she could not bring a gun into the country. My father had not heard of her shenanigans since mother had never told him everything. What to do? Well, we arranged for my sister, Janice, to take her to London to see the sights and let her shop for baby clothes and other things, gifts to replace those wedding gifts which she had kept. Bless my dear sister for staying with her and encouraging her to shop.

53

My sister and James' mother stayed at a fine hotel and ate at the best restaurants since my mother-in-law was paying the bill.

We had a double bed in the nursery so James' mother could stay with us and out of reach of my parents. Thankfully, she behaved herself by no excess drinking but I believe she continued to take her medicinal drugs.

Not long after my mother-in-law and sister returned from London, I went into labor. We called my parents and then the ambulance to get me to the hospital where I would birth using a hospital midwife. No husbands were allowed in the delivery room back then. I had a son and my father was over the moon having had no sons. He had a grandson to spoil and spoil him he did. It was the custom to stay in the hospital for two weeks, so new mothers had time to do more knitting for our babies, as back then we could not tell the sex of the baby ahead of time. So now I could knit little boy outfits in wool to accompany the other things that I had made, plus the knitted gifts from relatives and I have pictures of my son in these first outfits. My father gave James some time off so that he could be with me and our son. In turn, I did not have to worry about his lack of working and covering for him for a few weeks. My mother-in-law soon left for her home in St. Augustine and I for one began to breathe a little easier.

Remember in a previous chapter that I explained how my father hoped to buy a hotel using my hotel experience to help run it? Well, now was the right time to make it come true and with his first grandson, John, Father was ready to keep us all in England, even though he was not exactly thrilled with James as his son-in-law. Time would tell as we shall soon see.

FRENCH VINAIGRETTE

This classic recipe mentions 3 to 4 parts of olive oil to 1 part lemon juice or vinegar. Of course, additions can be added like garlic, herbs and to make it like the American version, add chili sauce, chutney, and even Roquefort Cheese.

Place in a jar to shake the following 4 parts olive oil, then add the following: ½ tsp. salt, 1/8 tsp. ground pepper, ¼ cup vinegar or lemon juice, ¼ to ½ tsp. prepared French mustard. Shake well (can add garlic).

KENTUCKY BIBB LETTUCE DRESSING

Great for a luncheon with a cold chicken breast or cold beef filet. Bibb Lettuce, 3 ½ tbsp. olive oil, 1 ½ tbsp. sugar, 1 tbsp. Worchester sauce, 2 ½ tbsp ketchup, 2 chopped hard-boiled eggs, salt and pepper to taste. Mix together. Pour over lettuce.

Chapter

6 THE HAMMERTON HOTEL

My Father took my husband with him to scout for the right hotel and found the Hammerton Hotel near York, on the main road between Harrogate and the old city of York. The place was a complete mess with cat urine all over the carpets and the grounds were a disgrace. There was a bar open to keep the license intact and where local farmers could drop in and have a beer. It was not the place to take the missus out for dinner but you could have a good old stomp around in your boots on a Saturday night when they had a local band.

Father bought the Hammerton and sold Pauline's Café but kept Ann's Café so that it would help defray expenses of the hotel. This allowed my youngest sister to graduate from school but she did not go on to college. Father was still into politics and, as I said previously, he refused the office of being the mayor because of pressing family business. He traveled a few times a week to Wakefield to go to Ann's Café, to see Mother, and take care of any problems. The journey between the café and hotel was only two hours, except in winter when it was snowing or foggy which took longer.

The hotel was not very large but it had nine bedrooms, a third floor with staff rooms, three bars, and a dining room that had been used for local dances or private parties. It was going to take a lot of time to get it back into shape. When the accountants came to take stock of the hotel contents, I took them into the dirty kitchen and pointed out that the dry food in the cupboards were sitting on newspapers over ten years old and would have to be discarded. The refrigerator was not in use but seeing that it had been closed for some time, it had quite a stench. When I climbed to look on top of this full size refrigerator, I found a long dead mouse. The cat apparently had not done his job.

We had chickens that had roosted in the trees because they were left to their own devices. So, there were no eggs unless you looked in the bushes and found some very old eggs that the foxes had not discovered. Father found a local handyman to make a hen house with a fence around it and then clipped the chicken's wings to keep them on the ground. I took care of the feeding and eventually they started to lay and gave us fresh eggs. Later, when we were finally in business, I used to go down to the hen house while the guests who were staying with us could see me out of the window gathering eggs. If the hens were not laying, I would buy eggs from local farmers to place in the henhouse and no one was the wiser. Anyway, they were still fresh eggs.

Father had hired a decorating firm from York called Hunter and Smallpage to decorate and furnish the entire hotel but before they could begin, and on our first day of occupancy, the previous owners had booked a Christmas dinner for a coach party. As it was close to that holiday, we felt obligated to cater the affair in that horrible dining room. We covered the room with a lot of cheap decorations, covering the bad spots, and then set about cooking a turkey dinner with all the trimmings. This was the first and last coach party that we would cater.

We hired two local girls to help, along with my young sister who was now old enough to work when she and mother came for the weekend. Mother always had her hands in something and was so money conscious that every time I turned around she was turning down the heat on my electric range. I had to ask father to have a word with her. Ann taught the local hired girls the methods which I had taught her, how to serve in the dining room, and to help in the bedrooms and kitchen. One of the girls was to become my young sister's friend and her sister became my baby's nanny since after all John was only a few months old. So, she took charge of him but brought him to me to nurse while I was whipping the hotel into shape. With two of the three bars now open, my husband worked both bars, especially when Father was in Wakefield. James was in charge and assisted by an older bartender who lived in the hotel's staff quarters. We used the third bar as a dining room for breakfasts for the residents until the main dining room was finished.

Soon we had new staff join us and they were from Ireland. When these girls arrived, they had very few clothes so Mother outfitted them and provided uniforms. She also arranged for the priest to pick them up early Sunday mornings to take them to church. Mother became their substitute mother and when they got homesick, she would comfort them. They were Catholic but afraid of priests so they would not confide in them, except for confession. Therefore, Mother became a substitute mother to them all.

When the hotel was ready for occupancy we opened with no publicity, just word of mouth, and we never had to advertise because that word of mouth was all it took. I was the chef and took care of the dining room as well until we were busy enough to hire more help. We purchased a beautiful revolving hors d'oeuvre cart just like a big wheel and a sweet trolley for a dessert cart which was just what I had envisioned long ago. These were great talking points with our guests since we were first in the area to have such elegant serving pieces. The only china that was in the hotel was in blue so we used this china with more additions for early morning tea service, breakfast, lunch and afternoon tea which was very popular on Sundays and consisted of tiny tea sandwiches, scones that we served with my home made lemon curd (recipe included) and pastries.

We traveled to Blackpool to purchase more upscale china, service for dinner plus silver cutlery and serving pieces, as we were to do full French silver service for all meals except breakfast. Suddenly, we became busy and I was slammed with walk in customers for afternoon tea. Father literally kidnapped two ladies walking from the train station on the way to their homes and brought them to the hotel to help out. This was our first encounter with locals other than bar patrons who were mainly farmers playing skittles, dominoes and darts, drinking draught hard cider or beer. These two dear ladies got busy hand washing the dishes, no dishwashing machine, then proceeded to wash my baby's nappies (diapers) and hung them outside on the clothesline to dry, not placed in the electric clothes dryer.

We were on the main bus route to York and Harrogate so there was always a bus outside the hotel, on the half hour going either way. The railway station was just up the road and the trains stopped every hour or so. They would drop off our newspapers and special French cheeses or other special foods that I could not get locally. Our German shepherd would go with Ben, the bartender, to do what we called the train run.

The ladies that father kidnapped were to remain with us as long as the family owned the hotel. Nana Ferguson was one hundred and three years and full of vim and vinegar, and Nana Kirby. These were the names that we and the children called them. The nappy service was offered free of charge to our guests. With the installation of showers in the bathrooms, we became well known to Americans from different European embassies as the hotel to stay at when visiting York and Harrogate. We offered nanny services, as I had a full time nanny living on the premises.

The menu was a Table d'hôte Menu which had lots of choices making it a six course dinner. Wines and other drinks were priced separately. Here is a sample of the foods offered for a fixed price. Hors d'ouevres available from the revolving cart with so many varieties to choose or take all. Hot Cream Soup or Consommé. A fish course such as Plaice Filet with a Sauce. An Entrée of Fresh Duckling a L'orange with a fresh orange salad (nobody did salads with the meal so this was unique). Roast Chicken with Tiny Sausages. Game Chips, Savory Dressing and Bread Sauce. Grilled York Ham with Pineapple, British mixed grill consisting of Filet Steak, Sausages, York Ham, Calves Liver, grilled tomatoes and mushrooms. Rump or Filet Steaks with all the tracklements. There was a wide dessert choice served from the Sweet Trolley. The cheese board with cream crackers was offered with all the cheeses of the world that had come on the train from London, then off to the cocktail bar for coffee and liqueurs or cognacs. We had a local butcher that slaughtered and hung his own meats and all our vegetables came from Colin Farrow, who brought the greens right to our door for me to pick and choose from, plus the best gooseberries and rhubarb for rhubarb crumble with custard, strawberries and raspberries for Sherry trifle and whatever else that was fresh that he thought I might like to serve.

Local salmon fishermen brought by their catch, to either cook for them or for me to purchase and cook for our guests. I got so tired of cooking salmon that I no longer want to eat it, so please don't invite me to dinner and serve salmon.

During shooting season, I had game hunters bringing pheasant, grouse and partridge which I hung properly until maggots were crawling all over them. I would pluck, clean and roast them with all the tracklements, as that's how the Yorkshire gourmet likes to have their game.

Mother and Ann joined us after the café was sold. Ann was now able to take over the dining room and leave me to handle the kitchen with more time to train new kitchen staff. Father and mother's friends would come dine with us including friends who owned big beer companies and they would stay at the hotel during the horse races in York as well as Doncaster. Since we did not have enough room to accommodate their chauffeurs, Nana Ferguson and Nana Kirby had them stay at their homes.

After a five course dinner, our guests would go to the cocktail bar (the old breakfast room) prepared for coffee service, so we could quickly reset the dining room for customers in the lounge bar who were drinking and giving their food orders, so that I could get cracking and be ready for them to come into the dining room all at one time. We had it down to a science and the customers raved about the food and more importantly, so many booked their table for the following week.

The back bar was used mainly by local farmers. It had a separate entrance and I would often visit this bar and chat with the locals. The lounge bar was where the gentlemen who were supposed to be walking their dogs were sitting around a roaring fire, smoking their pipes or cigars and the dogs were taking a snooze instead of a walk. One colonel was in dire straits as his dog had died and he had no excuse to partake of his Yorkshire Bentley's bitter beer. Have no fear as the colonel was back in the fold by dragging a small puppy into the bar and settling down to his usual routine. What the local male contingent did not see was the colonel carrying his small bundle, only putting it down just before entering the bar.

When the Christmas Season came upon us, Hunter and Smallpage decorated the whole place inside and out with fabulous, never before seen decorations. People drove from miles to see the displays and said that they had never seen such a show outside of London. Every alcove was festooned with moving collages all lit with fairy lights. The outside had lights twinkling in trees that you could see miles away. I remember much later seeing the outside of Tavern on the Green restaurant in New York which reminded me of our hotel. After the season was over the decorations were packed away for the following year but we kept the lights on the outside trees as this was a great landmark as to where the hotel was. I have a photograph of me working a buffet in the dining room which shows a little of the décor and another professional photograph of the dining room after it was completed in 1960.

One day my father's bank manager stopped by the hotel to see my father and give his condolences on the death of my husband's father. Apparently, James had been to the bank to get a loan so he could go to the U.S. to bury his father and did not want to ask my father for the money. My father knew that James' father had died long before we married and immediately demanded that James return the money which he did and told my husband to pack his bags and leave. James' went on the train to Harrogate to find a job but he did not stay long and ended up in London working at a hospital. I have no idea what transpired during this period but kept right on working at the hotel until James' returned just in time to take me to the hospital in Harrogate to give birth to our second son. James wanted girls and I gave him sons.

James said that his mother had pleaded with him for us to return to St. Augustine where she would provide a house and restaurant. So, with two small children and pram, we boarded the boat with hope for a bright future in the U.S. Knowing his mother, my husband and I should have known better and would soon experience how differently things would turn out as his mother had not changed and neither had we.

LEMON CURD

6 large egg yolks (no white) in a pan
Add zest of 1 lemon
½ cup fresh lemon juice
¾ cup sugar

Whisk all together. Bring ¼ lb unsalted butter to room temperature. Cut into pieces and hold until later. Heat lemon mixture over medium heat. Stir all the time (I like to use a wooden spoon till thick. Do not allow to boil). Take off heat and whisk in the butter pieces. Refrigerate. Good for a few weeks.

Chapter

7   WHAT COUNTRY ARE WE IN NOW?

Going back and forth between different countries, never quite settling down and feeling like a lost soul, I shall be honest at this point, after arriving in New York by boat, I do not remember if we came to St. Augustine by plane or train.

James' mother took us to a new home, manufactured by a company that she said was owned by her. The house was just up the street from where she lived. It was fully furnished and had a nursery for Paul with an extra small bed placed ready for the colored nanny housekeeper she had hired and was waiting for us. Paul had never seen a person of color, so he screamed bloody murder but I explained to the nanny who was patient and it was not long before both my boys bonded with her. She took them for walks in their pram, becoming a tourist attraction in St. Augustine, where lots of tourists visiting the oldest city in the USA took their photographs along with the more historical sights.

We went to "our" restaurant where trailer trains were right on our doorstep, so we attracted these tourists to our business. The restaurant was called The Village Inn and I still have the menus with what are now ridiculous prices for complete dinners which included juice, soup, salad, entrée, dessert and beverage. Some of the Entrée selections included Fresh Shrimp $2.40, Frog Legs $3.35, Lobster $4.35, and the most expensive was Prime Rib $3.60, just to mention a few. We were open seven days a week and I took one day a week to be with the children and cook for them as well as the nanny.

I remember one day I asked the nanny to sit with us for lunch but she refused as it was not allowed for a person of color to sit with white folk to eat. And, during this time of segregation, we never had colored people visit the café. When my children were brought in their pram to visit the café, it was ok for coloreds to sit with the children in the dining room but they could not eat. Our nanny ate in the kitchen where our other colored staff cooked for the customers.

I did not drive, not that I was afraid, but never had to. It was many years later when I was in Palm Beach when I finally learned how to drive with my bodyguard, Arnold, as my teacher. There will be more about him later in another chapter.

Unfortunately, James' mother had not changed and tried to take full control of our lives and business, ordering staff around and pretty much telling everyone that she owned the café and was therefore the boss. She knew nothing about how to run a café and actually drove customers away when she was either drunk or overmedicated. So, again, it was time to do the "moonlight flit" meaning leaving in the middle of the night to an apartment downtown with our children and all our things, taking nothing of hers.

James tried to get back into the Air Force and they refused him so he signed on with the Army. While he was away at basic training, we stayed at the apartment until he picked us up and took us to a camp in the Carolinas until ready to travel overseas. Once more it seemed we were on the run. James left for Germany with his unit while the boys and I went by military transportation to England to stay with my parents. My family was overjoyed, especially to have their grandchildren back and father had already arranged for a pony and instructor to teach John, who was now old enough to ride. One day Giles, the Welsh pony, escaped from his pasture, so there I was running down the main road trying to hang onto his tail with a coach load of American tourists busy taking photographs of this crazy English woman holding onto a pony trying to get it to stop. Well, Giles finally did stop after realizing that he had not made a clean getaway.

Now back at my family's hotel, I got busy tweaking the menu and teaching the kitchen staff new ideas. Of course, Nana Ferguson and Nana Kirby were busy as ever making the best Yorkshire puddings for Sunday lunch to go with roast beef as well as handing the sweet trolley, including the new desserts that I taught them which included Eton's Mess (recipe included) named after the Eton College.

John was now old enough to attend the two room schoolhouse in the village, which is now an historical building. He would ride his pony, led by Pam the nanny, and she was small enough to ride Giles back to the hotel until it was time to pick him up after school was finished. Our German shepherd was now older but still a protector of my children. His name was Peter and sometimes he would go to the school and do tricks for the children during their break but the children would not go back indoors so the teacher had to call my father and ask him to please take Peter home. My father would then hop into his Jaguar to pick up Peter in the open boot (trunk) and return to the hotel. Sadly, after some time, poor Peter was run over and killed by a crazy speeding driver. Father later bought Bruce, a Great Dane who ruled the lounge bar dog brigade with his head so high that he could look over the bar to survey his kingdom.

We received a call from my dear husband to say that he had found a place for us not far from the military base so we took a boat to Amsterdam, sending our luggage ahead, as we still had the pram and other things but had to leave Giles behind for the customers' children to enjoy. James picked us up in Amsterdam with a Volkswagen that he had purchased. After arriving in Southern Bavaria, we went towards a bar downtown from the base. We were now living on what was called the economy. James took us up stone stairs to what was called a cold water flat. One large room for sleeping, a small kitchen, bathroom and the place stunk of stale beer with a small heater in the center of the room. There was no living room. This was what he had arranged for his family to live in while he was on base or out several weeks working border patrol at the Czechoslovakian German border.

James could now get extra pay to house his family although I honestly wished that we had stayed at the Hammerton Hotel because we were not in line for base housing due to his rank. But, we were close to the base so when I was alone with the children, I would put them in the pram, go on base and do some shopping at the PX and the grocery store. There was a shopping bag that clipped onto the pram, big enough to hold many groceries, and another storage space to hold more stuff under the body of the pram where the children sat. I was an early bird, so I would often get the children dressed and go into town to do some shopping for sausages, etc. It was well noted by town residents that I did not show up with bobby socks on or with my hair in curlers like some women on base were known to do. I was also able to pick up the language, some I had learned along with French while in school, and I even taught John a few phrases.

Some of the German people were rude, they would spit on the floor as we passed and say bad things but I let them know that I understood their comments. They were even cruel to their own people. I remember when my husband was driving us downtown near the railway station during a busy period of the day and an obviously blind man stumbled, fell, and no one stopped to help him. So, I had my husband stop the car, get out and stop traffic and help the poor man up and escort him across the street. I got out of the car glared and gave everyone a dirty look but they just didn't appear to care.

One time when James was away on border patrol for a few weeks, our youngest son, Paul, threw one of his toys out of the open kitchen window from his high chair. I removed him to his playpen which was also his bed and began to run downstairs with John to pick up the toy. I fell down the outside steps, flat onto my stomach, and John was crying as he was scared to see his mummy unable to get up, but nobody came to help me even though the street was full of people. I managed to get up, outraged with these people who had no heart or feelings. I presume they hated still feeling like they were an occupied country.

I received a call from my husbands' commanding officer asking me to stop by and see him while James was on border patrol. James was a cook in the mess hall and the battalion had had a special birthday coming up. So, James, wanting to show off, took me to his kitchen and we got busy baking and decorating cakes with the emblem of the company on top. I also made home-style pies that the troops enjoyed as well as the commanding officer, who said that since James' family had joined him, his work was much better so he was upgrading him to sergeant.

Eventually we moved into a real apartment on base, fully furnished with three bedrooms. We were all much happier and I was pregnant with our third child. My parents came to visit us and we had barbeques on our grill. In England, no one had ever heard of real barbecue. It meant sausages on the grill. Now, all over the world barbecue is well known for its different sauces to slather on meats and everything goes on the grill. When Father and Mother came to visit us, we had barbeques so many times since Father loved the different tastes. Another favorite of Father's was a drink called Bolla, a concoction of different liqueurs blended together in a punch bowl, then a loaf of sugar soaked in rum is set alight after being suspended over the booze concoction.

As our third son's birth date drew near, we put John on the plane to be met by my parents in England. The national newspapers sent photographers and crew to take pictures and print an article as it was Councilor Stanley Tiffany's grandson. They had John sitting on Bruce, the Great Dane's back and I still have copies of the article. John had a joint passport with Paul but now Paul did not have a passport in our possession. After Tommy was born and a few weeks old, we managed to get a passport for the baby but poor Paul, whose passport was jointly held with John was now in England. So, Paul was to be smuggled out of Germany in the back of the car covered with a blanket and bribed with candy to keep quiet as we went through all the borders including France and then over the English Channel into England. All of this was done so we could get Tommy christened in our church which dated back to 971 A.D. After a short stay, we were able to safely return to Germany with all passports and children, as James' had to report back for duty on base. As long as he was in the military, there was no way to just get up and go, or he would have been court-martialed.

Not long after our return, I received a phone call from my sister Janice to say that our parents had been in an accident going over the Yorkshire Moors as a snowstorm and snow drifts had made driving bad. A driver on the opposite side of the road had plowed right into them. They had been on their way to my friend Margo and Terry's hotel called the Saltersgate Inn. This was my old friend from the Old Swan Hotel and her husband that was like a brother to me and the son that my parents had never had. The Saltersgate Inn was right at the top of the Yorkshire Moors and famous for its history of being a smugglers salt, not booze, pick up place. It had a fireplace in the kitchen with a fire that never, ever went out over the centuries, and was fed peat from the moors.

Without seatbelts back then, my mother had been thrown out into the snow and the steering wheel went through my father's chest. My sister Janice was now pregnant and our younger sister Ann, still married to her first husband, was also very pregnant and could not travel. So, my husband got special leave to fly the children and me to the hotel where my sister Janice and her husband were waiting for us, who began to tell us of news when the hotel phone rang and since I was at the reception desk, I answered it instead of the staff. It was Prime

Minister, Harold Wilson, on the phone, who said that if there was anything we needed, that we should call him at a special phone number which he gave to me and what a great message to tell my parents when I was to see them. I have a photograph of Harold Wilson with my father while having a teatime break during a meeting. Janice had everything in hand so we went in mother's car to the hospital, well actually Mother never drove but we all called it her car.

Both of our parents were in Pindersfield Hospital Wakefield where they were in different rooms. Mother had lacerations and had a broken thigh which meant that she would be in hospital for months because there were no quick fixes back then and she had her leg hoisted in the air on a pulley. Father had chest issues which my sister found out more about later and worse than initially thought. Since Mother was going to be a long time at Pindersfield, Father was transferred to a private hospital in Harrogate where friends stopped by, including the mayors of Harrogate and Wakefield. We even had a bar set up in his private room for liquid refreshments while important guests discussed politics, etc. When my friend Terry stopped by I asked him to talk to these VIPs and insist they cut down the length of these visits so my father could rest.

The hotel was busy and I was tired, so when Father was finally able to come home, it was arranged that I and the children would go to Butlin's Holiday Camp, a family-friendly place for working class families to have an inclusive, organized holiday. The reason this particular place was chosen was that it was close to the hotel. The Sun Newspaper published a photograph and article of the "Most Beautiful Mother and Child Competition" at the camp every week and always won by a girl never a boy. Well, I entered each of my boys with me and John was selected as the winner. I was asked why I had not entered Tommy in the Beautiful Baby Contest but I had thought him a toddler and was told by the judges later that he would have won. Golly, I was so amazed. We were in this nationwide newspaper and by this time my husband had been sent to Texas, so I sent him copies of the paper. My Mother, still in hospital, was absolutely delighted.

Mother did not like being in a private room and preferred other women patients for company. A piano was in the ward so when my Father was able to come every day to visit, he would play the piano and mother would sing. We brought lots of food from the hotel and shared with Mother's roommates so she was a very popular lady. Even though she was in bed in a very uncomfortable position, her voice was loud and clear. The matron of the hospital, head of all staff, even doctors bowed down to her, placed a new nurse in special charge of my mother, after all she was Councilor Tiffany's wife. This nurse, Brenda, was to become part of our family and to this day we all stay in touch with her. She became my sister Ann's best friend.

So James was in Texas which was fine by me as my love for him was gone due to years of infidelity and irresponsible behavior around my family and friends. I stayed married due to my upbringing and my country's feelings towards divorce. The fear of my Father saying, "I told you so" always stayed with me.

After Father was back on his feet, he began looking for another hotel since my sister Janice and her husband, Leslie, were happy to be back from Wales where both of them had lived and worked. They were now interested in settling down back home in Yorkshire where Leslie's family and all of our family lived. Janice gave birth to a baby girl and we were all thrilled.

My father received information from our brewery that the Expanse Hotel in Bridlington was up for sale, so we went, taking along the brewery official who would be instrumental in financial help, as the brewery was the beer supplier for the Hammerton Hotel. When we arrived at the hotel we were told it had sold that morning. Not wanting to leave any stone unturned the man from the brewery took us to look at the biggest hotel in

Bridlington, situated on three acres of lawn leading down to the Promenade and the North Sea. It was so rundown that all I wanted to do was turn tail and run as if I was in a nightmare. All I could think was, "Oh dear, what are we in for now?"

ETON MESS DESSERT

Served at Eton (probably the most prestigious English public school for gentlemen. Note that in England, public school means private school). Figure that one out!

Slice 1 lb. strawberries, add 5 tbsp. Kirsch liqueur. 5 tbsp. sugar. Hold. Beat 2 cups heavy cream thick. Hold. Purchase 1 bag white meringue and break into pieces. Mix meringue pieces, strawberries and most of whipped cream. Place in glass dishes. Place a blob of whipped cream on top and a strawberry. Serve.

Chapter

8 THE ALEXANDRA HOTEL

The Alexandra Hotel was situated on three acres of land, with a fabulous lawn sweeping down to the ocean but it was in terrible disrepair, never been looked after and showing its age. We went inside the damp, moldy Victorian hotel and I was saying to myself, "No, this is an impossible project," but nevertheless Father said, "Let's have a gander while we are here." I would have been more interested in the Expanse Hotel that had just been sold.

There were two bars at The Alexandra Hotel still open in order to keep the license intact. First, we went in the resident lift (elevator). Believe it or not it still worked but my heart was in my boots, worried in case it broke on the way up to the top floor where the staff lived. We were greeted by seagulls flying in and out of broken port-hole style windows. The furniture was so old that it was falling apart. However, I noticed some beautiful Victorian marble washstands complete with decorated wash bowls and there were a few other Victorian pieces including ornate toilet bowls in the bathrooms. Best of all were the decorated claw foot china bath tubs, all on pedestals and all the other three floors had these same pieces in the bathrooms.

The seventy five bedrooms contained beds, wardrobes, chests with drawers and bedside tables with a cupboard holding the guzunder (chamber pot) as there were no private bathrooms. At least they had washbowls with plumbing but it appeared the chamber pots had never been cleaned and, since the bedrooms had not been used for a few years, they were now unusable and should be thrown away. The dining rooms and other parts of the hotel had been closed (except for the two bars) for at least five years.

We began a tour of the downstairs, starting in the basement where the wine and beer cellars were situated. There was a stream of running water through the cellars to keep the wine and beer cool and this is also where we found the kitchen with a large stove embedded into the stone floor; everything was obsolete and I cringed when I saw it. There were plenty of other rooms here in the basement and probably used for offices. I could not wait to get out of this dungeon and walk up the stairs to the main floor.

Marble columns decorated the different areas of the lounges where the reception desk and public restrooms were. There was even a cloak room as the hotel was situated on the North Sea where it is almost always cold. Visitors, who had water instead of blood in their veins, would go for a quick swim in the frigid cold ocean, but we rarely ventured out without a coat. Next to the large dining room was what we in the trade called a still room, not a room to brew booze but to make tea and coffee.

No china, silver, pots or pans. In fact, it would take a lot of money for whoever bought this place. The dining room was empty as was the ballroom and front halls. At the entrance to the hotel was a revolving door. One of the bars was a cocktail bar run by Johnny and his wife. The other bar was called the lounge bar which also serviced the ballroom. In addition to the residents lift, there was another lift used for supplies to all floors and for staff to use so the main lift was for the guests only. When we were finished looking, all that I could say to Father on questioning me about what I thought was, "No, No, No," but to no avail as when Father says that we can do it, then, we shall get cracking and get this place ready for the season

The Alexandra had already received much publicity since it was the largest hotel and could be the finest in Bridlington. We had many inquiries and people calling for a brochure, so we took reservations to fill the first two floors and decided not to bother with the third floor yet, but picked the best bedroom furniture from all the rooms. A lot of it was antique and when cleaned and French polished it looked fabulous. Leslie managed to put new mattresses on top of the station wagon for us to sleep on as there was no way we could use the old ones. It took a few trips using all the transportation available to get everything to the apartment which we were to call home for awhile and it was located at the end of the first bedroom floor wing.

By now, Amanda was born to Janice and my boys loved her like a sister. We brought along our own nanny until we were settled in with the children and then hired a local girl for the position. Luckily, the apartment had fireplaces in all the rooms so we would be warm. The actual hotel was icy cold with some windows still broken letting in gale winds from the sea, so when we began to work, Janice and I wore our fur coats, fur boots and long pants to keep warm. The place was swarming with workers of every trade and we used the same firm, Hunter and Small Page, to decorate and refurbish like they had for the Hammerton Hotel. Since we were battling "Old Man Time," there were lights on outside the hotel allowing workers to work all night painting the exterior while other workers were busy inside.

My main problem was getting the kitchen transferred upstairs next to the dining room and the still room. It was quite a project but I was able to take care of it with the help of a supplier to the trade. I ordered all the china, pots, pans and silver from a company in Blackpool which Father took me to. After all, he was footing the bill with the help of the brewery. Everything was much the same as at the Hammerton but on a much larger scale. This time, we placed larger orders for the linens needed for the bedrooms, bathrooms and dining areas. My sister Janice was in charge of the bedrooms including hiring maids and Leslie hired a competent Maitre d'hôtel and he in turn hired his waiters.

My brother-in-law was a certified accountant and I believe he had handled the taxes for some Royals. He did, in fact, work for the government, but it was a secret position and he would not talk about it. He was in charge of all the accounts, the staff at the reception desk and generally helping where needed. Leslie interviewed and hired a head hall porter which is an important position as it is the first person of the staff to meet customers. He certainly looked smart in his uniform which included a jacket with tails and doorman's hat - a la Fred Astaire. Father came to the new hotel each week to check on progress and we held informal meetings to discuss staff hires and any other problems since most of Father's time was still spent at the Hammerton Hotel and political life. We were ahead of other hotels on the coast, including The Grand Hotel in Scarborough which was owned by the family of Charles Laughton, a famous movie star.

We installed a baby listening service so parents could switch on the system and the front desk would monitor sounds from the room where the children were sleeping. This way, parents could have their formal evening dinner in peace knowing we had a nanny working to tend to the little ones if needed. Another unique idea was to have special children's menus for supper trays delivered to their rooms as we preferred no children in the dining room during dinner service. Today, children are up much later and go almost everywhere with their parents, including formal dining rooms.

We had hired head porter who delivered newspapers to the guest rooms, leaving them outside for the maids to deliver when they served early morning tea. The porter cleaned the shoes that were left outside the guest's door when they were retiring for the night. He also tended the portable bar that was set up so guests could drink all night if they so desired but no alcohol was served to outside guests after regular bar hours, due to liqueur laws.

I was head chef to save money since the chef would be the most expensive member of the staff and I got busy creating menus. I had young commis chefs, chefs in training, which I taught to prepare the foods for the extensive set of menus. They were all males and I even pinched one of the young chefs from the Hammerton Hotel that I had personally trained. He was a great help since he knew my methods.

The breakfast menu consisted of a full Yorkshire breakfast including fruit juices, porridge and kippers followed by bacon, sausages, grilled tomatoes, eggs any style, baked beans and fried bread (bread fried in bacon grease), hot buttered toast with English marmalade and oodles of Yorkshire tea to wash it down. We could send any meal upstairs to the guest's rooms but most people preferred to go to the dining room for their meals and socialize. Morning coffee with biscuits (cookies) was served in the lounges where the general public was invited at a cost of one shilling; this repast was served at approximately 11:00 a.m.

Lunch was a four course meal, no soup and sandwich American style for our guests. A cart was rolled to the table with the hors d'oeuvre selection followed by the main entrée such as roast beef and Yorkshire pudding, steak and kidney pie, different choices of fresh Bridlington fish, crabs and lobster. There was also a cold buffet table filled with veal, ham and egg pies, other cold meat pies, York ham, cold lobster and crabs, just to mention a few of the daily dishes in addition to different salads. And, the rolling sweet trolley, just like at the Hammerton Hotel, with coffee.

Visitors could also have lunch, afternoon tea and dinner with us as long as they made a reservation. Hotel residents paid for their rooms which included meals so they did not usually miss a meal and as most of them were from Yorkshire, they intended getting the full value for their brass (money) even if they were worth millions of pounds. We were not a bed and breakfast hotel as there were plenty of these places in the town.

Afternoon tea was served in the front lounges with usual teatime treats. Hotel staff assigned to the still room took care of this meal and also the children's supper trays, allowing the kitchen staff to take a break before getting ready for the formal dinner meal served at 8:00 p.m. I stayed in the kitchen to prepare roast duck, pheasant, chicken, Guinea fowl, turkey or any other meat that would need a few hours to cook ready for dinner.

The dinner menu was more "Frenchifed,' if there is such a term, as that was the style of cuisine at that time when the hors d'oeuvre cart would be taken around with a more upscale and different selection than at lunch. The next course was the soup, and there was a choice of two, cream soup like Crème du Barry (a cauliflower soup loaded with Devon cream) or a clear consommé like Consommé Brunoise (beef clear soup with tiny diced vegetables). Now and then we had access to turtles so we made turtle soup served with a small silver jug of Sherry for the customer, to add to their taste. Today, it is an endangered species and no longer available. The next course was a fish course like Salmon Mousse for the cold fish dish, or maybe Quenelles de Crevettes (Poached Shrimp and Sole Dumplings served with Shrimp Sauce).

The main course consisted of one of the roasts that I had placed in the ovens earlier with sauces and garnishes. We offered British dishes including the British mixed grill which included filet steak, loin lamb chop, York grilling ham, pork and beef bangers (sausages) with mushrooms and grilled tomatoes, with the usual tracklements like H.P. sauce, horseradish sauce and mustard. The cold buffet table was similar to lunch with such cold foods as Chaudfroid Chicken Breasts (Cold Poached Breasts covered with Sauce and coated with Aspic Jelly), Cold Poached Salmon with Vodka Lemon Sauce (recipe included) Cold Quail served with Port Wine Jelly plus Dublin Bay Prawns with Dill Mustard Sauce or American Cocktail Sauce (this sauce was new to most guests).

Then came the sweet trolley with its famous Sherry Trifle, Chocolate Mousse loaded with brandy and lots of very decadent pastries, forever changing to suit the customer's tastes. We offered a savory course for those who did not have a sweet tooth, serving very British savories as served in the gentlemen's club way back when men dined at their club. We served Angels on Horseback (recipe included) and Welsh Rarebit, Scotch Woodcock (scrambled eggs on toast slathered with anchovy paste), topped with a rolled anchovy and garnished with watercress or mushrooms on toast (sautéed mushrooms served on toast spread with anchovy paste). In addition to the above, we offered a cheese board with various British and European cheeses with cream crackers, water biscuits and celery hearts. Coffee was then served in the lounge where a cart of liqueurs and brandies were served, not included in the meal price, or the resident's special tariff.

Our grand opening occurred on Good Friday and how we managed to do it I cannot remember but our fully booked hotel had guests coming through the revolving doors, followed by the head hall porter and his assistant, Vaughn, with their arms loaded with luggage. Leslie and his staff were at the reception desk ready to sign them in and escort to their rooms. No soft opening as they say in the business. We were hell bent for election, ready or not, and this was it.

Suddenly Janice and I realized the silver teapots had not been delivered to the hotel, so we made a phone call and heard they were on their way but that was not soon enough as the first guests who had arrived were expecting pots of tea as it was tea time. Quickly, we ran upstairs and retrieved three china teapots after rummaging through our personal belongings. The customers could not have cared less because everything else was in place including three-tier silver tea stands that held sandwiches and pastries. Our panic was over and the silver teapots finally arrived. But, just imagine a first class hotel without silver teapots. Gosh, what a calamity!

As busy and flustered during the opening as we were, there were very few problems and the whole family and staff pulled it off with many wonderful comments from our first guests. The baby listening service was a real plus for us; the nanny was kept busy with two babies in her lap, singing them back to sleep before putting them into their cots on that first evening. I was worn out but happy upon hearing comments about the food. We even had a family meeting with both Father and Mother about our first day's business, doubting if we would sleep a wink. Mother often came to visit us at The Alexandra, especially to enjoy tea with the grandchildren while staff at the Hammerton Hotel was quite capable and trustworthy but not so much during the weekends when it was busier.

We handed over the night's duties to the night porter who did a good business with his portable bar. We used small bottles of spirits, like the airlines, to make it easier for room service and for those in the lounges chatting and enjoying themselves. We could not serve alcohol to non-residents after the main bars closed and the last call for drinks was by saying, "Time, Gentlemen, Please."

Being the premier hotel in the area, we attracted different rock bands including The Moody Blues, Herman and the Hermits, and The Rolling Stones. These bands caused such a commotion that we had to hire security to stop groupies from getting into the hotel either dressed as maids or other staff. Seeing as we knew all the members of our staff, this tactic did not work and the culprits were taken downtown.

We opened the Alexandra Ballroom on Saturday nights for town visitors to come, visit and dance to our resident band. The lounge bar had a pass-through into the ballroom so holiday makers were able to purchase their own drinks or have tableside service. The place was packed and we became the place to dance with a real live band, not just a piano or organ. We also had a Wurlitzer theater organ on stage for the band to use and with Father being a natural on piano and organ, he played along. The bar sales were great, so busy that the wooden slats which we walked on to stop us from slipping, were soon ankle deep in beer but we plowed on. Even I worked this bar after I had finished with my other work and as my staff cleaned the kitchen before retiring. A lot of the staff lived on the premises.

I felt absolutely "jiggered," so worn out and we were just about to get through our first summer when we were asked to cater the Mayor's dinner dance. The hotel became known as the Alex to the locals and I wondered what Queen Alexandra would think of this. I have an old postcard with people in formal attire visiting the seaside for the day or even staying at the hotel. Quite frankly, I do not remember what the menu was for the banquet but it was a hit and then everyone went through the lounge areas into the ballroom. I do remember that I instituted a new idea. When the dancing was over, we served cups of consommé to warm the guests before they left into the chilly night for home. This was quite a talking point and we used the idea for many other occasions. That evening, I went for a walk along the promenade but I can't recall it at all. The staff later found me in a shelter on a bench and I was then escorted back to the hotel. The doctor was called and informed my family that I was on the edge of a breakdown.

My parents had friends who owned a hotel on the Italian Riviera in a beautiful town called Alassio, so they arranged for me to spend a fortnight, two weeks of being spoiled and spoil me they certainly did. One small problem, those who packed my bags forgot to include underwear in my luggage so I was able to buy all new underwear when I got situated. The hotel had its own private beach with changing cabins for each guest. After a dip in the warm ocean, I hung my wet suit over the cabin door and took a quick shower but suddenly it was gone. I popped my head out of the door and saw the beach master washing it and hanging it out to dry.

This man raked the sand as well as put a chair out for me with a small table each day. Every afternoon at 4:00, the beach master brought me a tray for afternoon tea with tiny sandwiches of Parma ham and Italian pastries with English tea to drink as well as fresh lemonade from the trees in the garden. With every meal at the hotel, staff brought a bowl of fresh fruit picked from the trees along with fabulous food. I never saw any pasta while there, that I remember. The meals were great and I had no stress, just a lot of pampering.

I took walks along the waterfront, shopping and listening to all the male singers that every restaurant employed. These bars and cafes were kept open allowing the breezes in the evening to cool the customers. I had pastries and a drink at a few of the cafés. It was a local male custom for unaccompanied ladies to be pinched on the "bum," the rear end, which happened to me even though I was wearing my wedding ring. I do believe it was a tourist thing. Older women were never accosted especially the local women wearing black widow's weeds. I returned home well rested, in good health and with a tan. Now, it was time to get back to work

I received a phone call from my husband informing me that the General, whom James' worked for as his driver, was allowing him a quick discharge since James told him that his family desperately needed him in the business. James was prone to telling tales for convenience and we were not too thrilled about it but what could we do? Leslie assigned James to be in charge of stocking the bars, with an office in the cellar but James soon made more of an appearance in the bars "chatting up" the customers with his American accent, especially young girls who frequented the ballroom on Saturday nights for the dances. Everyone was too busy to bother about what he was up to (including me) and after all, that was James, and the word Aids or other venereal diseases did not even cross our minds.

Now that the season was over, we devised a plan to hold black tie buffet dinner dances with a cabaret every other week. A lot of the town's many residents had not been to the Alex as most of them were too busy in the summer season, so this became a regular affair and we were always fully booked. It was held in the ballroom and we had tables and chairs moved from the dining room placed around the sides of the dance floor.

By now, thank goodness, we had hired a chef called Carter. A lot of chefs become heavy eating too much of their own good food but it was a different problem for me. I lost weight when I was cooking and the only time I felt like eating was when other people cooked for me and I did not smell the kitchens. Leslie would often "pop out" to the local fish and chip shop for some take out as a change from our richer foods. When he returned, Leslie would take the staff lift to the apartment so the smells were not wafted around our guests and I enjoyed this so much, always having a "good tuck in." My sister and I enjoyed ventures into town to shop and have a meal. It was also refreshing "not being on stage," and able to go to the hairdressers for "the works." Our hairdresser was the daughter of the brewery representative. Janice, Leslie and Amanda had moved to another suite of rooms along the hotel's private corridor, and James and I had the apartment with a balcony overlooking the wild ocean.

The champagne, cabaret, buffet, and dinner dances were still the big draw of the season and brought much needed income, especially when hotel rooms were empty. One time Leslie was looking for James and could not find him so I offered to locate him down in his basement office. I could hear noises coming from the wine cellar and found my husband having sex with one of the cabaret dancers. I quickly returned upstairs and informed Leslie and Janice. The cabaret dancer's father had accompanied her to the hotel, so I told him where his daughter was and he told me that she was, "Sowing her wild oats," which means kicking up her heels. To which I replied, "She is not going to sow her wild oats with my husband, so get her the hell out of here!" Of course, my family would not talk to James about it but it definitely left a bad taste in their mouths. My parents were not told of this, or of other episodes.

One night James left the hotel without saying anything and went into town. Sometime later, I heard a car approaching and as we had a balcony overlooking the driveway, I looked out of the French doors, watched and waited until I saw my husband step out of a small sports car driven by our hairdresser. (Remember, her father was the brewery director who originally showed us the hotel and was a good family friend by now.) When he came upstairs in the lift to our apartment, I went ballistic and try as he might, he could not explain his actions. I did not tell my family of this latest escapade and I would not use the hairdresser again. I told my sister that I was not pleased with her services, so I found another beauty shop within walking distance from the hotel.

James became bored being in one place and with so many family members aware of his conduct; he sold our share of the business to Leslie. To this day, I am unaware of the arrangement or of how much cash was given because Leslie, being a typical Englishman, gave James all the money for us. I did not want to get a divorce at the time as the children were still so young. Back in those days it was thought best for parents to stay together for the sake of the children.

Now, the traveling gypsies (we) were returning to St. Augustine, Florida. This time things would be different, or so James said, as we had the means to buy into our own business. I told James to go ahead of me, to get things ready and I requested that he take our son, Paul. My green card had long expired and since this card was my entry into the U.S., I needed to go to

London to renew it at the U.S. embassy. Traveling such a long way with three young and active boys "full of vim and vinegar" was a bit too much and I wanted James' help by at least taking charge of one of our boys. James had arranged to lease his deceased grandmother's apartment above what had previously been her large house and furnished it with what I thought was some of the money from the Alexandra Hotel. But, boy was I so wrong as you will soon see in the next chapter.

VODKA LEMON SAUCE

In blender, mix:
2 room-temperature large eggs
3 tbsp. lemon juice
3 tbsp. white vinegar
2 tsp. sugar
½ tsp. salt
1 tsp. dried tarragon
Pinch paprika

Blend all together, then gradually add (whilst blender running),
2 cups salad oil, 3 tbsp. Vodka

WELSH RAREBIT

1 ½ oz. unsalted butter
2 ½ cups grated Real cheddar cheese (not processed)

Place ingredients in a pan to melt over low heat with ½ cups
British Ale, plus 2 tsp. Coleman's prepared mustard (not dried).
Pinch salt & pepper. Low heat just to melt. Do not boil. Place
slices of toast in an ovenproof shallow dish, cover with cheese
mixture and broil until brown on top.

ANGELS ON HORSEBACK (FOR 6)

16 large, dried and shucked oysters
8 slices bacon (cut in half)
4 slices buttered toast cut in half

Wrap each oyster in bacon. Secure with toothpicks. Place under
broiler (on a tray). Turn once to cook bacon well, but do not
overcook or oysters will be tough. Place on toast.

Chapter

9 POSADA MENENDEZ RESTAURANT, FLAGLER COLLEGE

I left our two sons, John and Tommy, with my family at the Hammerton Hotel, and on my way to London where I had an appointment at the American embassy to rectify a situation I figured would be quick and easy. My father made a reservation for me at his friend's hotel, the Grand Metropolitan, and I was given the VIP treatment. Mr. Robert Maxwell was the owner of The Grand Metropolitan Hotel Chain and a gentleman. He had been a Member of Parliament with my father and the only Jewish member in Parliament at that time (and I was to meet his daughter much later on in Palm Beach). Unfortunately, Mr. Maxwell committed suicide after a scandal involving money and after much bad publicity, he apparently jumped off the back of his yacht and his body disappeared into the ocean. His crew heard a splash but did not realize what had happened until it was too late.

I arrived at the American embassy, had the same physical exam and answered questions that I had had when I first emigrated to the U.S. and explained how our son Paul was already back in the states waiting for me and I was taking our other two boys, who were U.S. citizens back as well. It seems that they were more interested in my education and degrees than the human factor but gave me the green card so I took it and left----go figure.

Across the street from the hotel where I was staying in London was a shoe store that belonged to Sidney's company. Sidney was mentioned in an earlier chapter and someone I had dated when I was single and working at The Grand Hotel. As I walked inside and browsed around, I was greeted by a saleslady and mentioned the fact that I was an old friend of Sidney's. She surprised me by saying that he happened to be upstairs in the office with the manager of this store. Sidney bounded down the stairs, hugged me and asked me what I was doing in London. I explained my circumstances and trip and by the look on his face, I realized that he still had feelings for me. Sidney told me that if things did not turn out right for me then I should call him and he would arrange for me and the children to come back to England. I must admit that when things looked gloomy for the future, I did think about what Sidney had said but had to hold myself in check since that would have been using someone that I admired but did not love. I never saw Sidney again and never, ever made inquiries about him.

The boys and I left by plane to New York, where James and Paul were waiting. Paul was excitedly telling us how he and his father had seen the Macy's Day parade from their hotel room apparently on the parade route and that they had eaten in some fancy restaurants while I wondered how much of the money from Leslie was used. But, at least Paul had a great time and therefore it was well worth the price because Paul had never previously had much time with his father.

My boys did not know much about baseball, American football, basketball or any boy games as I, being female and English "to bat" had no idea of these sports. So, I was unable to coach them. I hadn't even followed soccer, rugby or cricket in my country as I was the parent too busy working.

We arrived in St. Augustine to our furnished apartment above Grandma Master's house. James had bought the furniture, or so I thought, and we settled in. The boys loved the area being downtown and the two eldest "were able to ply their trades," shall we say, and my boys made perfect entrepreneurs. In the old slave market, tourists would stop and let local artists draw sketches of them. Now, these artists had competition as my boys would set up their own sketch easels and draw portraits just for tips so the tourists could not resist. John managed to get a newspaper route but decided he could do better than that so he decided to just plain quit. Tommy, the toddler, went into the garage and took out some very old newspapers, placed them in his little red wagon and tried to sell them to the neighbors but that was short lived as they "turned him in." The boys were able to get young pioneer costumes circa 1530 depicting the Spanish period, learned the script and took tourists around the ancient city explaining its history. Good tips were in that venture and I often wondered where they got all the savvy for these ideas.

I employed a colored lady called Adella. She was a lifesaver for me as she took over the house while I got on with the latest project called Posada Menendez Restaurant. James had found this fabulous restaurant overlooking the Matanzas River, opposite Castillo de San Marcos. It had been run by someone who "did a moonlight flit," by taking off without paying the property owner any rent. At least he did not strip the place of its furnishings. The property owner, upon learning about our experience, took a chance and we signed a lease. We made friends with a great couple, Peter and Donna and she would become my best friend for always. Donna did not like James later on, but at first she was ok with him and so was Peter. They put some of Peter's inheritance money into the business to become our partners. With just a few changes we were able to bring the place "up to snuff," including the placement of my piano on the enclosed porch area. We hired a blind pianist who taught at the Florida Deaf and Blind School in St. Augustine and a lady vocalist called Shirley to entertain customers. No jazz or rock music, just easy listening to enhance the ambience.

I reworked the menu to reflect the Spanish, French and British period during their conquests of what was the nation's oldest city founded in 1513. The following prices date back to 1968, and were in keeping with what I believed to be St. Augustine's premier fine dining restaurant, as most other dining establishments were low key. And, since the Ponce de

Leon Hotel was now closed and about ready to be transformed into a private college, there were no other fine dining restaurants around.

The following lunch menu shows just a few of our choices: Iced Gazpacho Soup (our recipe was requested by Gourmet Magazine) .40 cents, a cup of Jumbo Shrimp or King Crabmeat Cocktail served in a silver Coquille shell $1.50. Entrees included Arroz con Pollo (young chicken legs cooked with saffron rice and spices, Paella a La Valencia (shrimps, scallops, crab and chicken cooked in a paella pan) - both $3.00, New York Strip Steak with onion rings served on a sizzling steak platter $4.00. All the entrees consisted of house salad with our Posada salad dressing (recipe included) plus garlic toast (a very new bread alternative), Chicken Salad platter or Tuna Salad platter $1.75 with St. Augustine Shrimp Salad platter $2.25. Even the children's menu was a hit with the tourists, as the city was a big attraction and educational, so we had plenty of young visitors. For special- Kiddy hamburger with French fries, chocolate milk and ice cream $1.00. Pastries and Spanish Flan (flamed with 151-proof rum) for the adults. All for .60 cents.

For dinner, we did a lot of tableside cooking and quite "the talk of the town" as no one else did this style of cooking. I long ago realized that some of the better restaurants could be classified as being a theatre for the evening. Steak el Matador (filet mignon, shallots, mushrooms, spices and three wines, flamed with 151-proof rum) and Shrimp de Jong (giant shrimp cooked with wine and mushrooms plus our secret sauce, flamed with 151-proof rum) - both $7.25.

We used 151-proof rum for all flambé dishes because it does not need pre-heating, so no singed hair or burns, which is a very good tip for all your flambé lovers. For the French dishes we had Beef Bourguignon or Coq au Vin rouge $3.95. Seafood Newburg and all our lunchtime dishes with larger portions. We offered a vegetarian dish of Soufflé Omelet with Mushrooms

89

and Shallots - $3.95 - a vast change from the regular vegetable plate served in most restaurants.

All our entrees came with a house salad and Posada salad dressing (the recipe is at the end of this chapter) and garlic bread.
We had a tray of French pastries by the entrance of the dining room next to one of the flambé carts used for entrees and dessert. I think this set the tone in the evening, with the table candles lit and flames from the tableside cooking. Plus the piano playing set a very relaxing mood. We bought our French pastries from a pastry shop owned by our French friends who made authentic French pastries, and we had our own dessert including Spanish Flan Royale (egg custard caramel sauce and flamed just before reaching the table with the 151-proof rum) drama at $.60. Crepes Suzette (French crepes cooked tableside with orange, butter, sugar and Cointreau, and then flamed with Cognac) or Cherries Jubilee (bing cherries cooked in cherry liqueur flamed and served over ice cream), both $1.50.

We made Spanish Sangria (using Spanish wines, simple syrup loaded with fruit slices and served over ice in a large pitcher). Today, it comes in a bottle but not at all like the real thing at $2.50 a pitcher for two. Gaelic coffee, Turkish coffee plus Coffee Royale, American coffee and Sanka, now called decaf, after dessert. Quite a menu selection!

We opened for the season (summer is the season not like Palm Beach's season in the winter) for locals and tourists alike. We had an upstairs private dining room where we catered parties including a party for VIP's from Spain on a goodwill tour with the mayor of St. Augustine and the ambassador for Spain from Washington in attendance. Our food and service were well reviewed and we gave employment to many locals including the young people out of school for the summer.

90

We had a license to sell beer and wine but not mixed drinks or cocktails so we arranged for the owner of *Queen's Steak House*, over on the beach, to set up a bar on our patio and share in the proceeds of the sales. *Queen's* sent us a lot of business and we, of course, did the same for them. We advertised for *The Red Lion Tavern* on our restaurant's menu cover, where James visited so often that he even managed to get our kitchen help to cover his absences. Now and again, James helped wait tables, but Donna, Peter and I were much better at it and we pooled our tips to help cash flow but James hit the till so often and many times when he thought no one was looking. He never did it when I was keeping an eye on him but poor Donna and Peter were not wise about his tricks, at least not for awhile in the beginning. James handled the cash and it seemed that no matter how hard we worked and as frugal as we were the restaurant was not making money.

I was offered a job at Flagler College, formally known as the famous Ponce de Leon Hotel, as their food service director. It was at the time, an expensive, private Liberal Arts College for young women. There were scholarships for students who helped serve in the dining room clearing tables, etc. to pay for their tuition at $1,500 per year, their room and board another $1,500 per year, and which was quite a lot of money at the time.

There were Tiffany (Louis Comfort Tiffany) windows throughout the college, expensive Chinese urns, so large they were big enough to hide in and so many other artifacts that it made my head spin. I have always loved antiques and was used to seeing them in Britain and Europe, in addition to having them at the Alexandra hotel. In the college President's office, there were a couple of beaten up old rocking chairs and I wanted them. There were also boot polish marks on the marble chimney breast thought to have come from Henry Flagler's boots. I realized the chairs were of good quality, just in bad shape, so I plucked up the nerve to ask Dr. Carlson, the president of the college, if I might have them and to my surprise I was told,

"Yes," so I quickly got them home. They have been redone and are now in the safekeeping of my son John.

The college bedrooms, previously being hotel rooms, had fabulous furnishings. The college brochures stated the college "provided unmatched comfort amid magnificent high domed halls, art treasures and fine furnishings with a swimming pool, tennis courts and formal gardens... so you and your room-mate share a spacious room, deep carpeting, lounge chairs and your own telephone as there were no cell phones back in those days.

The dining room was "to die for" with all of its furniture intact; no need to change a thing in this high-ceilinged room. The students soon found my office through the swing door, from the dining room into the kitchen, and as I was not one of their professors they were able to sit at my table and chat, they having a soda and I, a cup of tea. They talked about boyfriends, family problems, and gripes about teachers so I became like a big sister to them. Some of the students on scholarships would babysit for me but of course as far as my boys were concerned, they were just their pals.

St. John's County Hospitality, comprised of managers and owners in the hotel and restaurant trade, decided to sponsor a hospitality training program for those who wanted to qualify for employment in the food service industry as a waiter, waitress, busboy, hostess or cashier looking for gainful employment. Normally an establishment which served alcohol was not able to employ people below 21 years of age, even as a dishwasher and this program kept the city's youngsters legally employed as well as helping all the hotels and restaurants that needed these young people's assistance. Flagler College offered their palatial dining room for formal classroom training with "yours truly" being the teacher. These jobs, for the State of Florida and the college kept Posada Menendez Restaurant afloat and a lifesaver for all of us. The program grew way beyond what I could ever dream about.

The board of education for St. Johns County asked me to set up the Chef's Culinary Arts Training Program, the first in the State of Florida, but there would be more to come all over the U.S. in the very near future, such as the Culinary Arts Institute in New York teaching high school graduates and other students of the rudiments in being a chef (no girls). In the morning, I taught students from the all-colored school, Hastings High School, and in the afternoon, students from the all-white school, St. Augustine High School.

Yes, at this time there was still racial discrimination in the South. I have a photograph of the St. Augustine High school students with me. Due to an initial lack of funds for this new venture, the boys wore uniforms from the Ponce de Leon hotel era and the college paid for their cleaning, so they always looked spiffy as you never knew who was to come and have a look at our program, visitors or guests from the governor to state senators. I was to write the book, so to speak, documenting all programs for future use and I was stoked, happy, to use my talents for this venture.

It was arranged for these commis chefs (apprentice chefs) to help prepare and cook meals for the students with other paid mature cooks to pick up any slack and take over during classroom lessons. Now, food preparation was not just food from scratch but utilizing frozen foods and prepared manufactured foods, as this was the wave of the future with convenience foods now coming to the aid of the mom and pop style places as well as Burger King and McDonalds, of which we had no knowledge of at the time, but these young commis chefs would definitely need these skills in such a diverse industry.

There were a few blind students in the program with their teachers from the Florida Deaf and Blind School, mentioned earlier in this chapter. I had never taught blind students before and found it challenging and rewarding. Many years later, I was to meet Jessie Torres, one of my students, who was working for Junior's restaurant in West Palm Beach. I read an article in the local paper about this young blind chef, so I called the manager of Junior's and arranged to see Jessie, asking the manager not to breathe a word so that I could surprise Jessie. I went into the kitchen and said, "What's with the moustache, Jessie?" and he said, "It's my Mrs. B." This was what everyone called me and of course my British accent certainly helped to identify me, and we had a good visit in the chef's office. Not too much later, Junior's closed and I never saw Jessie again.

So, the chef's culinary arts training program was in full swing but after a few paychecks from the board of education, I was asked if I was a U.S. citizen and when I replied that I was not, panic set in as it appeared the rug was about to be swept from under my feet. I had all my college credentials sent from England and assumed this was all that was needed but I was wrong. There was only one thing that would hold the program together and that was to get James certified as a teacher using his restaurant and hotel background to support this and the program was too important to lose for all of us. In addition, a swearing in ceremony was quickly arranged at the Jacksonville courthouse and I became the only new U.S. citizen sworn in that day. There were roses from the judge for me and when I returned to the college, the boys had made me a cake, not just for my citizenship but for my birthday. The entire college and all my students were in the dining room with streamers and balloons.

James now had an impressive teaching certificate, thanks to me. The program was saved and so were our jobs but I was still in charge of the program, documenting classes and teaching as usual but so tired of covering for James. One evening when I was working at the restaurant without James around, his absence not unusual, there were two customers who wished to talk to me. So, after taking off my apron, I sat with them and listened to their proposal. They wanted to hire me as the general manager

94

of Hy Uchitel's Voisin restaurant in Palm Beach. I told them that I would think about it and have an answer for them in the next few days. After the meeting, I did some research and realized who this person was. He owned the world famous Voisin in New York where everybody came to dine and now wanted me to run the restaurant in Palm Beach right on the ocean. I was gob smacked, to say the least.

That same weekend James' brother was in town with his wife and after I was finished working, I joined James, Jack and Joan at the Red Lion Public House where I found James busy dancing too close to a female who worked for the Chamber of Commerce, who apparently knew James well enough to bump and grind with him on the dance floor. My brother-in-law pulled my husband away from the dance floor and out of the pub in a hurry. Jack and Joan were embarrassed for me and I do believe that scene was the straw that broke the camels' back as now, I was ready for Palm Beach. By the way, James knew about the offer but thought he would also be soon employed at this famous restaurant, giving him more freedom for his type of fun as the saying goes, "when the cats' away the mice will play" applied to James.

The Chef's Culinary Association would later have its headquarters in St. Augustine and I believe they had no idea as to who started the first culinary arts program for young commis chefs. I held the designation of M.H.C.I. from Great Britain which meant, Master of the Hotel and Catering Institute, though the designation was discontinued many years later and I do not understand why but I am one of the few still alive and kicking in my case. As I have said time and time again that I BROKE THE GLASS CEILING before we knew what that term meant in the late 1950's and here at Flagler College, it was already 1969. I gave my resignation to Flagler College and the school board, knowing what would happen if James was left in charge as he had no skill in documenting or teaching and it was imperative to

95

find a qualified teacher for the program. They found the right person who then became James' boss.

I met with representatives of Voisin Restaurant and was offered very good wages with a room at the Carlisle Hotel next door to The Sun and Surf Condominium where the three room restaurant was located. When I left for Palm Beach, I knew the Posada Menendez restaurant would have to close as poor Peter was out of money without enough experience to handle it alone without me and with little or no help from James. So there went another venture and dream. C'est la vie.

POSADA SPANISH DRESSING

Slice 1 medium onion, very thin. Cover with 1 ½ cup red wine vinegar. Peel 6 oranges, sliced thin. Add to the onion mix.

Now add:
1/3 cup fresh orange juice
1 ½ cup olive oil
¼ cup white Spanish wine
Salt & pepper to taste.

Mix well with a whisk. Great on plain green salad lettuce.

GAZPACHO

Adaption of my original recipe requested by Gourmet Magazine, which was more labor intensive.

Blend together:
1 x 18 oz V-8 Juice
2 cups chicken broth (or beef)
1 ½ cups chopped green pepper
¾ cups chopped onions
1/3 cup lemon juice
1 tbsp. olive oil
Pinch paprika
1 minced garlic clove
Pinch salt & pepper

Blend until smooth. Taste, add more seasoning if needed.
Garnish: chopped scallions, peppers, onions, tomatoes, cucumbers and small croutons.

10 VOISIN PLUS O'HARAS

Peter drove me to West Palm Beach and "Aunt" Donna stayed in St. Augustine to take care of my children while we found out about the lay of the land. Adella, who was still working for me, would follow and work for me until I could find someone in Palm Beach to take care of the boys while I was working, but I had to find a place big enough. The Carlisle hotel was just a 'stop gap' for me and besides, Peter had to find a place for him and Donna to reside in as well.

Now, when you arrive in West Palm Beach, you have no idea where to go to get to Palm Beach, because there are no road signs, so we asked someone, "Where is Palm Beach?" At this time, there were no cell phones or any easier way to find out, so you asked. We were told to take any of the three bridges to enter this famous town known as Palm Beach. Taking one of the bridges, we entered what seemed the equivalent of Disney World for the rich because it was so well manicured and pristine. Not a blade of grass out of place or trash around but with plenty of police cars double checking as to who was entering the island. One thing about it being an island, the bridges could be closed if there were any jewel robberies from one of the world famous Worth Avenue stores or by ripping a woman's necklace from her neck. I would much later hire off duty police officers as security for a famous Palm Beach resident that I was to work for in a future chapter.

There was no parking of commercial trucks on the streets overnight and the garbage was picked up six days a week but not too early and no noisy lawn mowers or grass blowers allowed before 9.00 a.m. All deliveries were to be made through the service entrance of these estates, never to the resident and guest entrance. Most estates had very high, well-trimmed hedges surrounding the property, so no prying eyes to watch went on behind closed gates, and doors as well. Most people had at least one pool with a daily pool cleaner while the residents were in residence. A lot of service help to these fine abodes lived on the property or came to work from West Palm Beach by bus, car or taxi. There's much more in further chapters of the lifestyle of the residents of Palm Beach.

We drove to the front entrance of The Sun and Surf Condominiums which was right beside the ocean with a large pool and private cabanas for residents, and underground car parking so the hot sun and seawater would not cause damage to a Rolls Royce, Bentleys, Jaguars, Lincoln Town cars and Cadillacs. Upon explaining our reason for being there and given entry to the restaurant complex, we were escorted to meet the notorious Hy Uchitel at his poolside cabana, catching some rays and going over plans with his architect, Eugene Lawrence and David Theime, Hy's partner. I liked Eugene though I sensed something distrustful about David but kept a professional demeanor. Hy and I discussed my resume although he insisted that I was already hired as his advance head hunters had raved about me and bragged about my background, emphasizing my royalty connection as they were perhaps hoping to attract the Royals to Voisin. I was then given the grand tour of the three restaurant rooms, a private dining room for parties of twelve, the kitchen and what was to be my office, and there was a long bar as well as a piano bar. Each room was decorated differently; the main theme was that of Wedgewood blue and even the carpet was specially woven with the logo of Voisin dyed into the blue.

To get into this complex you had to come through the main entrance which had valet parking for guests. There was a slight ramp-style walk, going downhill with lit showcases on both walls, filled with jewelry from Van Cleef and Arpels, upscale boutiques like Gucci, Saks Fifth Avenue and Louis Vuitton, all with stores on Worth Avenue.

The Voisin New York was well known and Hy's brother, Maurice, owned El Morocco in the Latin quarter of New York, so the two brothers had a lot of contacts. The chef in Voisin New York was a fellow Englishman, Richard Clark, who trained under Escoffier and had been at Voisin for thirty four years, until he retired.

Hy had hired a French chef for this new Voisin called Louis, who had a very quiet, even temperament unusual in many kitchens today. Louis and I hit it off, each having respect for one another's knowledge. The resident pianist was Ralph Strain and our host was Pepito Rousseau, brother of Lily Pulitzer, the famous designer. Why a host instead of a Maitre d? Well, Pepito knew all of the "Who's Who in Palm Beach," spoke many languages and made a very handsome appearance in the rooms welcoming every lady with what was known as the Palm Beach kiss which was not a kiss but a slight non touch on each cheek. Arnold was the cashier who would end up later as my bodyguard. All of these men were talented artists doing many sketches on scraps of paper for the guests. I have many sketches of me, as a memento of our time together, by all of these artists whom I called my friends.

The Voisin coffee shop had two chefs from the Stage Door Deli in New York, now kept busy with breakfast and lunch. This place was frequented mostly by residents and also kept busy with room service and cabana service. Some of the items on the menu could be ordered at either meal: juice, half grapefruit, figs or stewed prunes with cream for $.75. Appetizers were Gefilte Fish, Herrings in Cream Sauce, Hot or Cold Borscht with Sour Cream or Boiled Potato all for $1.00. Lots of egg selections including Nova Eggs and Onions $2.00, Wheat Cakes $1.50, Corned Beef and Eggs $2.00, Pastrami and Eggs $2.25. Salads including individual cans of Tuna, Sardines, Salmon with Green Salad $2.25 and for entrees, Gefilte Fish with Boiled Potatoes, Stuffed Cabbage with Boiled Potatoes, cheese blintzes with sour cream or franks and beans for $2.45. Chicken in the Pot, (recipe included) Brisket of Beef with Potatoes or Chopped Steak and Potato or Vegetable $3.50. There were lots of sandwiches starting at $1.75 and desserts $.75, tea or coffee $.25 with Sanka and milk $.30. Breakfast and lunch only as this kitchen closed at 3.00 p.m. By the way, the way I have told you about the menu was just the way it was printed - simple, no frills.

The Chinese Room was decorated with the same blue décor except for banquet seating and the chairs were covered with animal pattern material, like El Morocco. The Chinese kitchen had all the requirements needed to cook that type of food, including huge woks and a steam oven for the famous ribs. All the rooms and entrances had fabulous chandeliers and vases in Wedgewood-style china and ashtrays. I have both a vase and an ashtray as a memento.

The menu for the Voisin Room was a Prix Fixe, a set inclusive price of $11.50. Appetizers were a choice of Shrimp Cocktail or Terrine du Chef, Avocado des Gourmets or a soup like Turtle Soup with Sherry, Vichyssoise or Onion Soup or Madrilène en Gelee. Entrees were Pompano Veronique (Poached Pompano with Grapes on a Cream Fish Sauce), Cote de Veau aux Morilles (Veal Chop with Morel Mushrooms), Poitrone de Capon au Champagne (Capon in Champagne Sauce) and Entrecote de Beef Marchand de Vin (Steak with Red Wine Sauce), all served with Vegetables and Salad plus various ice creams or Chocolate Mousse, coffee or Sanka. Crepes Suzette for two was $3.50 extra or Soufflé for Two was $4.00 extra.

An a la carte menu was offered after the trial run and was a very extensive menu but we needed to open, not quietly but as easily as possible, allowing waiters' time to give their clients excellent service right from the start.

One of the residents living in the condos was Zsa Zsa Gabor. Another very fine lady was Madam Alexandra, a famous doll maker whose dolls were apparently well known except by me. With three boys, I had never had an occasion to purchase these dolls but upon meeting her and seeing some of the dolls in her apartment, I noticed each doll had the likeness of her face. She enjoyed my company and thought my accent was charming, so she invited me for tea in her apartment and gave me a doll called Rosebud. On another visit, she gave me a small doll in Scottish dress. I still have these dolls but they have been well loved by the little girls who came to see me. I did not know until much later what the value would have been if Madam Alexandra had signed them but I doubt if I had known this fact that I would have had the impertinence to ask her. These dolls are ready and waiting for my granddaughter Allana to cherish.

Many times when working for famous people I was asked, "Did you ask for their autograph?" and I always said, "No," as I did not think it proper. When word got out via Pepito and by newspaper articles, even a few with articles and photographs about me, reservations rolled in and we were busy. Voisin could not legally advertise as the restaurants were in a condo and Hy had not figured on this so later it would take its toll.

The "Who's Who" of Palm Beach came to the Voisin including Jim Kimberly of the Kimberley Clark tissue fortune and his very young wife, Jacqueline, whose later divorce hit all the newspapers and TV. It was very steamy and involved Peter Pulitzer, grandson of Joseph Pulitzer, the newspaper publisher, and his wife of the moment, Roxanne. Both the Kimberly's and the Pulitzer's were friends at this time and both parties would dine together and sit around Ralph's piano, drinking champagne. Pepito's friend was the manager for Van Cleef and Arpels Jewelers, and he escorted Ann Light, ex-wife of J. Paul Getty, the famous billionaire, to the Voisin, so that was the reason for the showcase of Van Cleef and Arpels. Of course, Ann Light and all the other ladies came well decked out in fine jewels. Brownie McLean was a regular with her entourage of fun friends. She was the widow of Jack (Jock) McLean, who flitted away his family fortune but had a small inheritance from his grandfather until his death. Brownie used her talents as a party thrower and organized world trips, being compensated and enjoying life to extremes.

There were two sisters whose names I cannot remember but they used to come together to the Voisin room. Their faces were painted white, so garish and ghostly but this was Palm Beach and anything goes. So many famous people that I could not keep count of them all but left it up to Pepito and Ralph to point out who was who.

My mother came to dinner at the Voisin and met Hy for the first time. I took off that evening for a change so I could dine with her and let her see what the place was all about. With all of Mother's experience and knowledge, she was used to top notch service and food, having dined all over the world. She had been a guest of worldwide ambassadors, presidents and royalty, due to Father's political business, and would have made a great food critic.

Hy did what restaurant owners should never do which was that he kept coming to the table, asking over and over again how the food and service was. For restaurant owners, waiters and hosts to repeatedly ask is annoying. Please just ask once. After guests have had time to taste the food, check and then leave them alone to enjoy their food. Hy kept calling my mother, Lady Tiffany, which was embarrassing for my mother as she never called herself this name at all and he also made sure that he said it loud enough for all the tables around us to hear. He sat and chatted with us and said the meal was on him, and so it should have been as we were never left alone to enjoy it as mother and daughter.

The Sun and Surf was the first Jewish condominium to be built in Palm Beach as there was, and still is, discrimination with certain clubs not allowing Jews to join or even be guests in their exclusive club. The strange thing was Voisin, having a Jewish owner, was different because most of the clients in the Voisin room or the Chinese room were not Jewish, except for the coffee shop, which as I said catered more to the residents of the condos. The same could also be said of Maurice Uchitel at the El Morroco in New York. I had never heard of the "Jewish problem" and guessed it was far away from this area, but Hy talked about kikes and explained to me what it meant. I tell you I was gob smacked to hear him talking about his fellow Jews this way.

Donna finally arrived with Adella and the children. I had rented an apartment on the top floor of the tallest building, over the water in West Palm Beach on Flagler Drive. It overlooked Palm Beach, called Norton Park Towers next to the Norton Art Gallery. Today, it is still there but next to much taller apartments and condominiums. Donna and Peter decided on an amicable divorce, as Peter felt like a fish out of water in Palm Beach. He left but went on to manage a Denny's restaurant in West Palm Beach and eventually remarried. We would often go to the restaurant for a late meal as this Denny's was open twenty-four hours and we often felt like breakfast after a long night working.

There was an honest to goodness diner in Green's Drug Store. It was the local and only diner in Palm Beach, opposite O'Hara's and St. Edwards Church, where the Kennedy boys would hang out with local workers to eat great diner food in a much laid back atmosphere. I would often go for a bite to eat on my way to Voisin and there would be Hy and the gang chatting over coffee and donuts.

Donna took care of the coffee shop and had other duties but Hy wanted to pay her under the table which was apparently how it was done in New York. Donna had words with him so he fired her and was thus black balled from the restaurant property but as she was my driver, she would wait outside for me until I finished work. A very good customer, Bob Mentser saw Donna waiting for me outside and when she said that Hy would not allow her inside, Bob took her by the arm and escorted her to the bar. Well, when Hy saw this, he could not say anything because apparently Bob had a lot of influence. Bob would often bring Donna in for dinner and as he owned quite a few bars in Palm Beach County, he employed Donna full time. Donna rented a great apartment on Coconut Way near the Chesterfield Hotel in Palm Beach, so she was quite comfortable.

James came down a few times and was upset because he had lost his prestige at Flagler College and, quite frankly, I had had enough of his tactics. He insisted that I place our two oldest boys in military school, Tommy was too young. Adella was getting homesick as were my boys and it was not long before I took my tearful boys out of military school. I found a less expensive place to live and as my mother was coming to help me, we found a house close to local schools. Upon moving, I had a visit from the police department with instructions to have all my furniture picked up as James had not made payments on it. Here, I had thought it had been paid for out of the proceeds from the Alexandra hotel. I managed to keep my piano, made a deal to keep the dining room set, and let them take the rest. Thankfully, unknown to James, I had a few dollars that only my mother and I knew about, so I went shopping with the children for a new set of bedroom furniture. It was in the latest style with patriotic covers and pillows, so they were happy. My dear friends gathered furniture they did not need and also asked their friends and relatives for contributions.

That was the end of a long and often unhappy marriage and I knew it would be up to me to support our children. After the divorce, James had problems paying child support, was twice thrown in jail for no support and his mother came up with a thousand dollars each time. I still have judgments but there was no point. I was used to working hard and capable of making a good living for us and with mother's help I kept going.

Once, James asked my mother to bring the boys to Tallahassee as he said that he missed them so much, so Mother talked to me and I told her to go, as she was feeling sorry for him and wanted to somehow rectify the marriage for the children's sake, so off they went. Not long after they were gone, my mother called to tell me that James had a woman named Joan living with him and that she had a little girl. Remember, we had been told so many times that James wanted a daughter. Mother was to return but not with the boys as I was looking for a new home for us. I received a call from Joan telling me to pick up my boys as she was leaving James. I had a car but had never driven alone for such a long distance but I made it. I went to the house where my boys had been left alone while their father was working and they came running into my arms with all of us in tears. The milkman came and asked for Mrs. Billington whereupon I said, "You are talking to her right now." His jaw dropped as I was not the Mrs. Billington he had been doing business with.

When James arrived home from work as a cook in the university kitchens, I had some strong words for him and told him that I needed to leave the boys with him for a few more days until I found an apartment; at which time he was to take them to the Greyhound bus station, place them in care of the driver and upon arrival at the West Palm Beach bus station, Mother, Donna and I would pick them up. The boys were clinging to me, especially Tommy, as he was so young, but I calmly explained that it would be only for a few days more and they should hold on to one another until I called, which I soon did with good news that we had an apartment with a swimming pool and lots of other boys to play with. So they were returned to me with poor Mother upset at having believed that James wanted his family together but all the while living with a "new wife."

At Voisin, we had a secretary, Barbara, who gave birth to a little boy but she was so sick that she had to stay in the hospital. Donna and I found someone to watch her twins and another daughter, who were actually her step-children. My mother volunteered to take care of all the children including Michael, the baby. Barbara was Jewish but not her husband.

Hy needed an accountant so Barbara brought in Dick, who was soon to be my second husband. Dick was very debonair, well-dressed in grey slacks, and like all Palm Beach men, he did not wear socks with his loafers. As my friend Jan later asked me, "Pauline, was this lust or was it love?" I had presumed at the time that it was love but I was wrong as future chapters will show. Hy was not happy with the situation as Dick was not divorced and besides, Hy had other plans for me that included getting the Royals, as they were called, to visit Voisin.

The Duke and Duchess of Windsor were coming to dinner with a party of twelve, so we prepared Voisin's le quatre cent room, which was the small private dining room. I should explain that this Royal couple was notorious for using their name and title, rather than spending money, which in turn gave their hosts bragging rights and for a charitable fee of about $1,000, one could have their photograph taken with the Windsor's. In England, I would not have dreamed of using my friends, Prince Richard and Prince William like that. Well, when the Duke and Duchess were to arrive, Hy suggested that he and I meet them at the door and when I was introduced to them that I should give a deep curtsy. I told Hy that Edward was not my King and she was not my Queen, therefore I would not curtsy. Hy was fuming mad, but I agreed to stand with him and welcome them as the manager of Voisin. When the Duke and Duchess did arrive, Hy stepped forward, bowed to them and said, "Please, your Royal Highness, may I present my manager, the daughter of Sir Stanley Tiffany, Miss Pauline Tiffany." All I could do was nod my head but after they entered the private dining room, I told Hy that this was not right and I did not appreciate the phony introduction but he fluffed it off and said I must make more of an appearance in the room. I was so mad at being used that I refused. So, Hy fired me as I was of no further use to him, not playing his stupid game. I had over $4,000 dollars in his safe though he refused any knowledge of it so I left kissing my well-earned money goodbye.

I often wondered if the chef, Richard Clark from Voisin New York had really been trained by the most famous chef of all time, Escoffier, and whether or not Hy paid him under the table. Voisin did not survive, perhaps due in part to no advertising and trouble with vendors. In New York, it may have been easier to procrastinate paying vendors but in Palm Beach, it was a definite no-no, so he left town in a hurry.

Across the street from the Sun and Surf Condominiums was the well known O'Hara's Night Club and Restaurant owned by Vince and Marjory with their family. The Kennedys and all the prominent people in Palm Beach would drift in there after the balls were over. The revelers in full evening dress, and tourists would drink and dance until 5:00 a.m. when the place closed just long enough to get it cleaned and then re-opened for the regulars.

Donna and I knew Vince, having met a few friends there after work. When Vince heard of Hy Uchitel's deeds, he enquired if I might wish to take charge of the restaurant part of O'Hara's, as his brother and sister-in-law were in the midst of a bad divorce and since Helen was in charge of the restaurant, he was at a loss. I was offered the same salary as what I was supposed to have received from Voisin, so I accepted the job until their family problems were resolved. Dick was not that happy at my taking this job because it would put me in a different light being around too many men. I did not perceive that this was anything other than being protective and he hired Arnold to accompany me where ever I went. So, Arnold quit

108

Voisin to watch over me at O'Hara's, driving me, and even taking my mother and boys out shopping. He was an older man in his seventies who had lost his fortune gambling but so happy to be accompanying me, a younger woman, as he hoped people would think he was my sugar daddy but after a while he, too, was becoming possessive of both Donna and I, so we became uncomfortable. I asked Dick if I could learn to drive and Arnold taught me. Dick arranged for Kledi, a friend of his, to give me an older car that she had and there will be more about dear Kledi in another chapter. Here I was, after all these years, driving. Donna had her job and no need to chauffeur me anymore.

At O'Hara's, Palm Beach socialites had late suppers in the dining room which served steaks with the O'Hara salad and their famous dressing but when the chef quit, poor Vince was in a panic until I went into the kitchen and was soon able to fathom the recipe, writing it down for the next chef and making a couple copies for Vince, just in case. The recipe is with this chapter. I remember the night when the ex-governor came to supper and I did not call him Governor Kirk, just Mr. Kirk. Boy, did he set me straight about this mistake. When my father was no longer a Member of Parliament, he did not use the designation, therefore I wrongly assumed this with Governor Kirk, and so I said to myself, "Pauline Tiffany, you had better learn this new protocol."

O'Hara's was the hang out for the New York Mets and the famous Don Drysdale tried to date me. The bartenders had a bet, unknown to me at the time, that I would say "No" and of course the bartenders won the bet as I was madly, though I should say mad, in love with Dick and besides I knew nothing about this game of baseball or the fact that these guys were stars.

The younger members of the Kennedy clan were regulars as well as Senator Ted Kennedy. The O'Hara's were Catholic and right next door to the premises was St. Edwards Catholic church where both the O'Hara's and the Kennedys worshiped.

At O'Hara's, the Kennedys behaved themselves, not like what was reported they did in other bars which made headlines and talked about all over the world. I remember after the balls were over and every one wafted towards O'Hara's, the Kennedy clan would get hungry for a late supper and always ordered a steak sandwich with house salad (and my dressing).

Dick was a now a regular at O'Hara's and even James showed up trying his best to reconcile in spite of all I had been through with him. He soon had a live in relationship with a woman called Joan. I could not have cared less as I do remember his excuse to stay married was the fact that he would be embarrassed going to the convention in Miami without me. By the way, he married Joan, divorced her, remarried her and their relationship is one of being back and forth.

Helen was soon ready to return to work, so I thanked Vince who knew that I would still visit as a customer and it did not take long before I was given employment as an outside catering consultant for the well known Chef John Bennett.

O'HARAS SALAD DRESSING

In a bowl add,
2 cups mayonnaise
½ cup sour cream
½ tsp. Italian herbs
½ tsp. garlic powder
½ tsp. dried parsley
Pinch salt and pepper (to taste) and add enough milk to make the dressing pour thick. The Kennedy's loved this dressing and took some of it home.

VOISIN MADRILENE EN GELEE (COLD GELLED SOUP)

Serve in small glasses with a plate underneath (e.g., Glass Punch cups). Boil together and then simmer 3 cups chicken stock, 3 cups tomato juice, 3 crushed garlic cloves, 3 tsps. Sugar, 2 small chopped onions, 3 tbsps. Chopped celery, 3 tbsps. Chopped chives (if using dried, then half the amount), 2 tsps. Worcester sauce, 2 tbsp. lemon juice, salt & pepper (can easily add more later).

Taste for flavor, then strain into a bowl. (I use cheese cloth for this, or use triple paper towels or paper coffee filter).

Soften 6 tsps. Plain gelatin in a little cold water. Leave for a moment to gell, then dissolve over hot water. Now add to the consommé and stir.

Have a tray ready to pour the consomme' onto. Not a bowl when it is set (after being in the refrigerator). You chop it all up into small pieces and place into the glass dishes. Sprinkle a little chopped fresh parsley just on the center of the top. Serve with crackers or good French bread and butter.

Talking about butter, I have the pet peeve about restaurants serving ice cold butter pats that can't be spread on the warmer (or cold) bread or crackers.

*The Duchess of Gloucester
with Prince William and
Prince Richard*

*My father,
Stanley Tiffany, M.P., C.B.E.*

*Jan Masaryk, Minister of Foreign Affairs of Czechoslovakia
(& son of the 1st Czech President) with my father*

l-r Prime Minister, Harold Wilson, with my father and Barbara Castle, M.P.

The Alexandra Hotel, Brindlington, England

The Alexandra Hotel

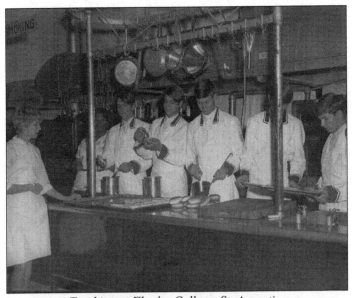

Teaching at Flagler College, St. Augustine

*Posada Menendez,
St. Augustine, Florida*

*Bon Appetit Cooking School,
Stuart, Florida*

*Bon Appetit Restaurant,
Stuart, Florida*

Dining Room, Bon Appetit

*My Catering Videos "Profitable
Catering Made Easy"*

1ˢᵗ Place Menu
Competition for
Bon Appetit

Photo used for Kiplinger's
Changing Times Magazine

The daisy arrangement Rod Stewart & I made for his home

Mr. Hurbaugh

*Golf cart donated to the
Martin County Fire Department,
by the Hurbaugh Family*

Mr. Berndt "The Old Salt"

At the Peslar's

*"Most Beautiful Mother & Child" Competition with my 3 sons
(John, Paul & Tommy)*

*The Village Inn,
St. Augustine, Florida*

*My son, John, with me
having won 1st Place in the
Competition*

The Hammerton Hotel (I am 2nd from left)

The Hammerton

The Hammerton Hotel near York, England

C'Est Ci Bon, Palm Beach, FL

Chapter

11 JOHN, CATERER TO THE 'ROYALS'

John Bennett was a great chef, especially when it came to off-premises catering. However, his manner of dress and demeanor needed some professional polishing when he was trying to sell Palm Beach parties, so that is where I came in, to put a little finesse in the business.

He realized that he fell short when trying to sell his parties and wondered why, so he asked me to go along with him. I soon figured it out but did not want to offend him so I told him politely that I could do a better job of promoting and selling his parties and said that he should do what he knew best which was cooking. Contracts were required with a 50% deposit to secure the date and to ensure that John had up front working capital. Also stated in the contract, the balance of the bill was due at the conclusion of the party, since previously, John never had a signed contract and ran the business by the seat of his pants. Bartenders, butlers (this was the terminology for waiters) and any special staff were to be paid separately and the hired help were responsible for their own taxes. When I sold a party, I always required a date and confirmation of the number of guests by three weeks prior to the party.

I would not throw in meals for bands, entertainers or any other help that was not with John Bennett Catering. I made a note that remaining, uneaten food could be placed in the host refrigerator, but not if the food had been sitting out of refrigeration as John could be sued for food poisoning; top notch caterers had already been sued. The Breakers Hotel had this trouble and they were a large company with deep pockets but John was a small business and could not survive with any bad publicity or a law suit.

Now dressed in a smart business suit bought from one of the consignment boutiques in Palm Beach which sold gently worn clothes from ladies who had maybe worn the garment one time, wearing Ferragamo shoes, and carrying my Louis Vuitton briefcase, I was ready to go. Apparently my British accent was perceived as upper class although I thought that I had a Yorkshire twang, like fellow Yorkshire woman and best-selling author, Barbara Taylor Bradford and I would use when we were talking together, and then have to interpret for other people.

My first visit for a party enquiry was to Mrs. Flagler Mathew's home. It was near her grandfather Henry Flagler's home, now a museum, to discuss with her and her social secretary a menu for an afternoon tea party. I asked about her likes and dislikes, so that I could please her and her guests. She soon realized that being British, I knew exactly what a real afternoon tea was about, not just finger sandwiches, punch and mints as we laughed about this notion. I took notes and arranged to meet with her three days later, allowing me the chance to confer with John and draw up a contract. I mentioned that I had worked at Flagler College as food service director and ran the teaching program for young chefs after it had been converted from her grandfather's Ponce de Leon hotel. I even mentioned the two rocking chairs from her grandfather's office that I had been given, and after mentioning this, I thought to myself that maybe I should have kept my mouth shut as she may want them back but she was glad that I had restored them instead of throwing them out.

Back at the office, John and I discussed the menu, costs, etc. and what we should propose. He agreed although it was more money than he would have asked, and it was also agreed that I would be there to supervise the party. I bought a velvet tuxedo from Sak's Fifth Avenue which spent more time in the dry cleaners than any other article of clothing that I owned. This tuxedo was soon to be well worth what was spent on it as Mrs. Flagler Mathews introduced me to a few of her guests, most unusual but great for business. The tea party was a great success and I was to receive more business from this charming lady.

I was now on a roll but dared not let a client come to the office as it was in a bad part of West Palm Beach and not a show place, holding catering equipment for the business just thrown here and there. Organization was not John's strong point and I requested his catering trucks be parked out back, as he was used to leaving them out front to attract business until I told him that this was not a good idea as clients may knock on the office door and see what a shambles the place was. Most of Palm Beach would not dream of crossing over one of the three bridges into West Palm Beach except to go to the hospital, morgue or airport (none of these places were allowed in Palm Beach) so that was not a problem.

One particular party that I booked was for a heavy crane company owner from Canada who lived in a large house opposite the ocean and they had, like many oceanfront property owners, an underground passage to their private beach with cabanas bigger than most regular homes. I was met by an English butler and taken to meet the lady of the house in the sitting room to discuss a menu for a new years' eve party for approximately 200 guests. She requested ice sculptures in pink and in fact the whole party was to be in pink with pink champagne, pink poinsettias, pink napkins and special rented pink china plates.

I like pink but when it comes to pink plates for the food, I personally would not have chosen it for the menu she picked but this was her call. Beluga triple zero caviar to be placed in an ice sculpture of a mermaid carved from pink ice with condiments of chopped egg, onion, and lemon placed around the tail. I do not like to have triple zero caviar contaminated with onions and egg because this is such delicate caviar and the most expensive but this seems to be the in thing for certain people not used to the service of great caviar. Lots of cold canapés, which were to be butler-passed, consisting of Pate de Foie Gras and Pate en Truffe on Toast Points. A chef would be hired to shuck oysters at a special oyster bar where the oysters, huge shrimp, lobster bites and crab legs (no shells) were set on ice and condiments placed in silver coquille shells. There were also hot hors d'oeuvres too numerous to remember but all were made in the kitchens of John Bennett, not like today where these are massed produced and taste nothing like the real McCoy. These too were passed by the butlers.

A large buffet table was draped with pink net skirting over white linen to keep the pink netting subtle and special background lighting was used to accent the food that chefs were to carve for the guests. I suggested filets of beef kept warm in a sizzle chafer be served with tiny pumpernickel rounds and a pineapple glazed ham with liqueur and hot turkey breasts carved for sandwiches. This was going to be an expensive party, especially as it was New Years' eve, so the price was also going to be higher.

I went back to confer with John and determined the price per person, much higher than any party that John had catered before and when I delivered the contract, it was signed with a 50% deposit up front and the remainder of the bill to be paid at conclusion. Even John would work at this affair wearing his chef whites, and I, of course, wearing my tuxedo. Strange, but if people tried to remember the caterer and forgot the name, it was referred to as the caterer that had this English girl wearing a velvet tuxedo. I knew now for sure that the tuxedo was a show stopper and we would be remembered.

I kept getting calls to say that the number, slowly but surely was going up, so I asked John that maybe I should get a further deposit to bring it up to 50% but John said no as the local sheriff was to be a guest in addition to some Arabian sheiks and other notables, besides this was for the company owners hoping to promote their business.

When we arrived to setup for the evening, I was informed that the sheiks were up in the turret room sitting on cushions and would not be coming down in the elevator to mingle until later. I therefore arranged, with the consent of the lady, to have a butler take care of the upstairs turret room with everything, but no pork since it is considered unclean to religious Arabs.

The party was a huge success but the sheriff was not in attendance, nor quite a few guests previously named, although I personally knew from other catered parties, that it was not unusual. John was busy loading the catering trucks at the end of the party and I took the final bill to the lady who sent me to her husband. When presented the bill, he told me that it would have to be sent to his offices in Canada, not even the help was paid and no matter what I did, I could not get a check from him. John had already left for the office and no longer in contact with me, no cell phones back then remember? So, I had to leave the bill with this man and left for the shop with my tail between my legs, hoping the check would soon be in the mail. Yes, really! But, it didn't come.

I stopped by the house a few days later to learn that apparently the house was only rented for six months. I did not call first, but was once again met by the English butler whom I had personally taken care of with plenty of food and champagne, as he was a fellow Englishman. I was told that madam was not at home but he would tell her that I had called and as I began to leave, the butler came outside to tell me that she was there but neither he nor any of the other staff had been paid so they were all hanging out as at least they had a place to stay while hoping their pay would soon be resolved.

From what John's attorney gathered, the only company that did get paid was a jeweler on Worth Avenue for jewels bought for his girlfriend, not his wife, so the wife would not find out about his infidelity. Now the famous detective, Madam Pauline was on the case, so I called all the beauty shops in Palm Beach to ask, "Is my dear friend a client there?" Bingo! I found the right shop without a problem and made a nail appointment at the same time as hers, not to be divulged to her, as it was to be a surprise.

The sheriff's bailiff, with writ in hand, followed me to the shop where I pointed her out. Talk about a shock! She, I swear, must have got her knickers in a knot, as the English expression goes, to see me with the bailiff in tow. I quietly left with madam's evil eye following me out of the door. I wish I could report that justice was done but they flew the coup back to Canada and we never got so much as a sausage in payment because they went bankrupt.

I managed to get John's company advertised in the "black book", a social index directory where all the names of the crème de la crème of Palm Beach WASPS (white, Anglo Saxon Protestant) were listed and by which hostesses could check to see whom they should invite to their soirees. Names, addresses and phone numbers were in this book even if they were not listed in the regular phone book. I had never heard the term WASP used before I came to the U.S. but I guess that was because I was one. Wow, how lucky can you get! The advertising really helped with John's catering and in having my name and degrees listed in this "bible". We now had access to people looking for a caterer as we were the only caterer in the book.

I went to visit a couple who were to entertain for guess who? Yes, the *Duke and Duchess of Windsor*. My knowledge of correct protocol and previous experience with royalty, gave me no problem in booking the party. I was not the only caterer called to submit a quote but I must have impressed the couple with my confidence and knowledge.

125

I arranged to have a tent on the lawn, hung with lighted chandeliers, and stretching over the pool area. It was to be covered by wood flooring then carpet, except for an area designated for dancing to the internationally famous Marshall Grant Orchestra, the king of swing of the Palm Beaches.

The party was a black tie event with a formal sit down dinner. Guests were instructed not to fawn over the Windsor's but to take the cue from the hostess as to what she wanted to happen. The Windsor's were on their royal best behavior. As I mentioned in a previous chapter, if you wanted to impress people in Palm Beach, then invite the Windsor's but be willing to pay big time. Now, I was actually seeing the Duke and Duchess in action without being forcibly introduced and pushed forward with comments regarding royal connections, as good old Hy Uchitel, my old boss from the closed Voisin Restaurant had attempted to do without my consent or cooperation.

Cocktail hour was precisely one hour and then the guests sat down for dinner. Dinner started with my recipe for cucumber vichyssoise with tiny cucumber sandwiches (recipe with this chapter), Florida pompano amandine as the fish course, then the entrée, roast filet of beef with chanterelle mushrooms in a red wine sauce, white asparagus and potato rosettes. A simple salad was served European style, after the entrée, then chocolate profiteroles for dessert which was apparently the Duke's favorite. No cheese course or sorbet. Coffee was served and the champagne kept flowing.

After much dancing, which of course, the Windsor's danced together and then with their host and hostess, the party came to an end by the signal that the Duke and Duchess were leaving for their bedroom suites, and their hosts were left to say good night to the other guests. As usual, diehard party goers retreated to O'Hara's restaurant and bar to see my old boss Vince for their usual night caps, as the evening was young by Palm Beach standards. It gave guests time to brag about their dinner with the Royals to all those who had not been invited. Maybe they would make it home before the milk man came, except the milkman was not welcome in Palm Beach. After all, he made too much noise with his bottles clanking and this was not London with Eliza Doolittle dancing all night.

CUCUMBER VICHYSSOISE
(Serves 6)

2 Cucumbers – Peeled, seeded, and chopped. (Reserve 6 peelings from one cucumber and set aside for garnish).
1 Pint Buttermilk
¼ cup fresh parsley
2 Scallions, chopped (only the whites)
1 Pint Sour Cream
1 Tsp. fresh dill (or to taste)
2 Tbsp. lemon juice
½ cup whipping cream
Salt

Place ½ of the diced cucumbers in a blender with ½ (quart) of the buttermilk, and blend. Add chopped fresh parsley, chopped scallions and blend. Add rest of cucumber slices. Pour mixture into a large bowl and fold in remaining ½ (quart) of buttermilk. Fold in 1 pint sour cream. Add fresh dill, salt, and lemon juice. Fold in ½ cup whipping cream, gently. Refrigerate until cold. Garnish with peeled cucumber slices. Serve with cucumber sandwiches (see Chapter 3 recipe).

Chapter

12 BON APPETIT COOKING SCHOOL AND CATERING

Dick and I were married, very quietly at his dear friend Kledi's house in Jensen beach with her minister officiating. The only people present, my dear friend Donna and my two youngest children. Kledi was a widow, her husband had worked as a captain on a huge boat which plowed its way through the Great Lakes, and out to sea for ninety percent of the year. Kledi told me that she and Peter had had a platonic relationship, therefore no children, as no sex.

Dick took care of all Kledi's finances, like he was her husband, and she never questioned what he did with her pension or savings. We took a short honeymoon and visited his son Dean in the state capital of Tallahassee, Florida and to see property that Dick owned at Deerpoint Lake. To get to the property, you had to drive along a dirt road, over two rickety bridges and then straight through the St. Johns Paper Company property until you realized that you had now left the heavy growth of trees and through a clearing to the lake property. Dick said it was forty acres of land with some water covering the land from long ago. He also said that he had papers proving that Captain Morgan's treasure was somewhere on the property.

Dick's plan was to get his son Gary involved in the project he had in mind, as he loved the outdoor life and this was right up his alley. They would build wood cottages to rent and have a convenience store for supplies. This was one of Dick's many dreams but the only way to get to this property was by going through the property of St. Johns and I wasn't too sure that they would love people tramping through their forest of virgin trees with their camping gear and maybe set the place on fire. And, another thing was the county did not allow any camping right on Deerpoint Lake, so the building of septic tanks for waste was not about to happen. Consequently, this project was put on the back burner.

Kledi had a real estate license, under Dick's ex- father-in- law, and had heard that there were four waterfront properties on the market with a monstrosity of a house set back on one of the lots, so she purchased them for her and Dick, to stop Dick's ex-wife from getting them. She never said that the property was a joint venture but always called it Dick's property. Even she was brainwashed before I had ever reached the scene but as time went on I could see the pattern emerging. Back in Stuart, at the estate-zoned property, we found out this strange house was built by a man who had thought that Cuba was going to bomb the U.S., so the house was built with 14-inch solid steel re-enforced block; it was just like a huge box with no character at all.

All the waterfront properties were situated on the St. Lucie River and overlooked Stuart city hall, though you could not see the water with all the dense undergrowth and tall pine trees. The property was cleared and ready to develop. At the same time that Dick was renovating the house, he was building Kledi a new house across the road, on railroad tracks, so she would not be close to us. Please note that it was on the railroad tracks and not on one of the waterfront plots.

Dick thought that he could divide the property into three lots, with the house being set back, his idea was to sell the waterfront lots at a big profit but the county would not accept this idea as the land was estate zoned and not able to be divided into three different lots. The best that he could do was to split the property with the house from the waterfront. Then, he was able to sell to a couple who wanted to build their house on the water and moor their seaplane in front of their house. Down went another one of his ideas. The county and city were wise to this man who carried a briefcase and boasted about having an architect's easel in his bedroom. He finally sold the other properties but what he did with the cash was never told to me, and I knew better than to inquire.

Now, Dick was drinking so much that it was scary. He had become physically as well as mentally abusive. As far as anyone was concerned, I had a few accidents and hit my mouth as well as my throat. Thank heaven for turtle neck sweaters. I remember once after he tried to strangle me that I ran across the street to Kledi's house and showed her but all she could say was that she was so sorry for me.

My boys kept away from this happy home as much as they could. Now Tommy was staying away from school and ended up at the District 2 Fire Station, telling the Chief Ed Smith, it was teacher's planning day and asked to help washing the fire trucks. It seems that most every boy's dream when young was to be a fireman and Tommy was no exception. He quit school and worked as a dispatcher for emergency services. Martin County then was an all-volunteer fire department and in the middle of the night, Tommy would take off on his bicycle, then later his motorbike and much later his car when his alarm system went off waking the whole house.

Dick said that Tommy was on the wrong track and should stay in school, but boy was he wrong. My youngest son would become, as I call him, "the big cheese" meaning the big chief. My son took all of his high school equivalent courses and now has a master's degree after all those years working his way up the ladder, no pun intended, to become the most respected Martin County fire chief and at such a young age. You see, there are some happy moments in my life!

Dick still had clients down south in West Palm Beach and there was Judy in Palm Beach who had been a friend and client of his for many years. He more or less advised her how to handle her money as she had no children or other legal advisers.

130

I mention Judy because she loaned him the money to fix the monstrosity of a house so he could put in a cooking school, permissible in the estate zoned house, and since I was a certified teacher, I could therefore teach classes in gourmet cooking. The cooking classes would then be written off as a business expense. This was a unique concept and a feather in his cap. As for me, I was just the teacher and he the owner of the business and property. It took such a long while to renovate. He hired two men from West Palm Beach who were very good workers but it took forever as Dick kept making changes. Eventually it was finished and I was instructed to purchase everything that I needed from Barbara, the ex-secretary at Voisin, who now owned a cookware store in the "Tony" Harbour Bay Plaza as her husband had purchased Queen Palms from Dick's land in Pahokee.

Dick ordered brochure covers and I prepared them by typing in the classes and prices and mailing them to people who had seen my one time advertisement in our local Stuart newspaper. I did really well with demonstration classes, showing how to make the foods with hints and tips that the students enjoyed just as much as the cooking. Then, I gave the recipes for everyone to take home.

Most of my students were women and a high percentage of doctor's wives but I did have a few gentlemen. One gentleman was a baron who had a Rolls Royce and an oriental chauffeur who would disappear for 2 ½ hours while the baron was in class. Two other gentlemen came together for every class and they were real cut-ups who loved to cook. One of the doctor's wives said that her husband was against butter, so she bought sticks of margarine just so she could wrap her butter sticks in the margarine papers and he was none the wiser. I tell you the devious things women can get up to.

Classes were mainly demonstration but for certain methods such as making egg rolls in the Chinese classes, everyone joined me for hands on training instead of watching me in my demonstration mirror. Classes always finished with tasting all the dishes and sipping a glass of wine. And, since classes were mainly taught in the morning, I advised people not to make lunch plans as they would not be hungry after the session.

Cooking classes were unheard of in our area with very few in the country at that time. Of course, there was Julia Child on PBS who really helped get everyone interested in learning how to cook gourmet cuisine. Because I taught cooking classes to students in the workplace for so many years, this was an easy transition for me and a wonderful outlet for my otherwise friendless life.

There were two women from Tequesta who came for classes but I soon found out they were going back to their cookware shop using my recipes and methods to teach their own cooking classes. I told them they were no longer welcome and even my students thought it terrible to pick my brains like this.

There were a couple of ladies from Vero Beach who had never cooked in their lives because both were from wealthy families and already had cooks in their kitchens. These ladies desperately wanted to learn how to cook and this was also good business for Barbara, who was ready to outfit their kitchens.

When I taught Chinese wok cooking, nobody had a wok or tools, so with Barbara's help we outfitted their kitchens with Chinese cooking tools. Back then, it was not easy to get Chinese food supplies, so I had to place an order with a local Chinese restaurant for such foods as dark soya sauce, oyster sauce, egg roll skins, bok choy cabbage, fermented black beans, dried Chinese mushrooms and sesame oil, just to mention a few.

Some of my students asked me where they should store their woks and I suggested they wrap them in paper and store under the bed which they did if they lived in a small apartment. These woks were made of heavy rolled steel and I explained how to season them; to never use soap or scrub too hard since once they are seasoned they can be used for years without foods sticking and use less oil.

I even taught kitchen hygiene making sure that everyone washed their hands well before touching food in my kitchen, and to never put a knife in the sink as someone is bound to slash their fingers. Many ladies had long, varnished nails but you would be surprised at how many of them cut their nails short and soon not wearing polish, just like me. When I was working I never touched my hair or face and always kept a bowl filled with water, in which I placed small teaspoons for me to taste the food, as I would never dream of sticking my fingers in the food.

In one class, I demonstrated how to bone and cut up a chicken, with the carcass ready for the stock pot whereupon I added vegetables and bouquet garni, a cheesecloth bag of fresh and seasoned herbs, and then cooked slowly for hours until all the flavors of the chicken were absorbed into the stock. Naturally, I made a batch of stock ahead of time as class was only for two hours. The following week, one of the ladies told us that her stock tasted so good when on the stove but when she strained out the stock over the sink, she neglected to place a bowl under the strainer and all of her beautiful stock went down the drain.

One of my pupils from Vero Beach had problems with cutting up a chicken so she came early and before the others arrived I showed her the technique again. She asked me if I could somehow piece it all back together as she was entertaining a gentleman for a Chinese dinner which she would prepare while he was there. I put all the pieces together with toothpicks and wrapped it up for her to take home, unbeknownst to her friends in class. This would have been a great success except that she used three cups of long grain rice to only one and a half cups of water so the rice became bulky and sticky to which she added more water until the pan was full of rice enough for an army. The gentleman guest had a good sense of humor so the evening, and maybe the night, was a success after all.

I let my students bring a guest if there was room, so one lady brought her daughter who was married to an Argentina cattle baron, for my class where I demonstrated how to make bread with a food processor, as food processors were the latest new gadget. I made the bread dough, showing how to proof the yeast, then after the dough had rested and allowed to rise (I had made a triple batch earlier), I made a loaf of bread, sticky buns, bread rolls and cheese bread with my dough, so we had sort of a brunch style tasting, with wine of course. This delightful young bride also came to a few other classes with her mother (bread dough recipe with food processer included).

A few weeks later I received a call from Argentina with a question from this same bride saying to me, "Pauline, you taught me how to cut up a chicken, so now how do I catch it, kill it and clean off the feathers?" I shall not go into details about this blood chilling method, for those of you with sensitive stomachs, but I explained it to her in detail. She sent me a photograph of her bread rising and one of the breads ready for eating. Never did see the chicken.

Three of my ladies who were doctor's wives requested a cooking class to include their husbands. I set up the dining room for the meal, using my fine China and silver cutlery. My son, John dressed in his waiter outfit, ready to serve the meal in French silver style after all of the dishes were cooked and presented on silver platters ready to eat. When the party arrived I gave them all aprons and asked them to wash their hands. The men were doctors and scrubbed their hands as though they were getting ready for surgery. The menu was of their choice and the Entrée was Roast Duckling a la Orange with Grand Marnier Sauce. One of the doctors made a fine julienne of the orange peel, so precise that I should have taken a photograph. They brought their own wines and I made some of my petit chocolate truffles to accompany coffee. The appetizers, soup, fish course and desserts were all dishes that we had done in our cooking class, so the wives had the upper hand on this.

Although worn out watching eight people using sharp knives, it was great fun with my eyes darting back and forth watching and helping them all make a great evening's entertainment. I did teach my students how to use knives in my regular classes but this was not the usual class.

Dick was basking in the limelight at what he took credit in creating from my talent. He would audit my classes, watch me and take notes. I dreaded these classes, but no one else knew that he was mentally abusing me by keeping me tense and uptight. After class was over and everyone was gone, he would tell me that I should have done this or that, and I should listen to him since after all he had been a trustee at Atlantic University in West Palm Beach. I never disputed this fact and tried not to argue because it would have made him mad, he would have had a few more drinks and I was fearful that he would take it out on my two youngest sons, so I always kept quiet and my sons never knew.

Remember, I had already been divorced and at the time there was stigma attached to a divorced woman. We always used to whisper in my country, "She's divorced you know." And, Dick would tell me that no one wanted a woman with three children since, after all, my first husband did nothing to support my children. Dick had his favorite watering hole where he could be found every day. When I used to hear him coming up the stairs, I kept my mouth shut as he spewed insult after insult at me and I never said a word to anyone. I just smiled. I was a prisoner at his whim and unless you have been in this place there is no way that you can understand. Go ahead and say, "Why would a woman with so much knowledge and talent put up with

135

this?" Well, you get brainwashed into believing that you cannot make it without him and your children would suffer, so you keep your nose to the grindstone, head down, and keep going, putting everything you have into your work, even though you are not the owner.

The cooking school was a great success and after four years there were more cooking schools all over the country. One or two of my students had been to other schools and flattered me by telling other people that this was the best, not just for my thoroughness, but for all the hints and tips they received.

Some people wanted me to cater their parties but we did not have an authorized kitchen for catering, so Dick had a bright idea. He had property on US1 that had been used for an auto body paint shop, so he had the insides gutted with the help of my sons and other workers and put in a catering kitchen with the front set up for a gourmet shop. I needed to find refrigeration and for special counters so I scouted newspapers for sales of commercial equipment that could be utilized with few changes to fill my needs. This project was going on during summer as I did not hold cooking classes in the summer since a lot of people left for Europe or traveled north to the mountains away from the humid, hot sun in Florida. By the time the winter season arrived, cooking school started again with a catering division ready for business and Bon Appétit Gourmet Food Shoppe, filled with foods unobtainable anywhere in our area.

Upon entering the Bon Appétit Gourmet Food Shoppe you were greeted by two huge dolls called Sherry and Brandy, who looked like ladies of leisure sitting at a table with a glass of sherry and looking around to see who was coming in. Children loved these dolls when visiting with their parents who were looking to purchase food for their parties. There were two freezers full of flash frozen gourmet foods and these goodies were made by me with the help of my son, John, and a flash freezer of -25 degrees, which stopped ice buildup. Everything was made of fresh ingredients including eggs, pure butter, and cream. I had a prepared assortment of hors d'oeuvres for last minute cocktail parties that a host could place in their oven for about twenty minutes, such as Petit Sausage Rolls (which were not pigs in blankets), Crabmeat or Chicken Profiteroles, Escargots Bourguignon Phirozhkis, Petit Ham or Mushroom Cream Puffs and Chinese style Chicken Wings, as well as a variety of my pates from my famous Chicken Liver, Apple Cognac and Cream Pate to Duck, Grand Marnier and Macadamia Nut Pate.

For a quick gourmet meal, I made meals such as Chicken Breast Dennison, Seafood Newburg Crepes, English Steak and Kidney or Steak and Mushroom Pie, Beef Bourguignon, Coq au Vin rouge and even Italian Manicotti all made from scratch. Desserts consisted of Grand Marnier Mousse, Lemon Frozen Soufflés, Mocha Liqueur Gateaux, even fresh homemade pasta and stocks to help a hostess create a meal fit for a king, and nobody need know that she had not been slogging, or busy in the kitchen all day. I now had my own stock of Chinese and Indian goodies for the cooks.

After cooking classes were over, everyone made a trip down US1 to buy their goodies. Son John was now fully involved and serving over the counter and, with his acquired knowledge of cooking, he was able to advise the customers.

Dear Kledi was a whiz at making Scotch eggs. What are Scotch Eggs? Well, we hard boil fresh eggs, shell them, wrap in a mild sausage meat, flour them, egg wash and roll in fresh made breadcrumbs, refrigerate and then deep fry to cook the sausage meat thoroughly, cool and serve. For cocktail parties, I cut them in six and place with other cold canapés on trays. The British eat whole Scotch eggs in pubs with their beer or on picnics with salads as it is such a versatile food with so many ways to utilize them. I remember one time my mother telephoned me from England and asked, "What are you making now?" to which I replied, "Scotch eggs." She laughed as I had always, in her mind, been the French gourmet style chef so never in her wildest dreams did she associate me with British food. I told her the Shoppe shelves were filled with such things as Bird's custard powder, pickled onions and British drinks like Ribena. I brought my children up on this childhood beverage and even have a photograph of my son, Tommy, falling fast asleep with his bottle of Ribena at his side.

Now we had a kitchen and premises to do catering. The first party that we catered was for one of my lady students from cooking school. Please understand that Stuart was still a small town and the kind of catering previously done was home-style or bought prepared food from the grocery store so they were not used to my style of catering.

Mrs. Peggy Matherson asked me to cater two supper buffets on November 3rd and the 16th in 1979 and I have the menus right in front of me as I write, so let me give you a taste of the menu for these first catered parties in the sleepy town of Stuart. There were 45 guests for each party and as I explained in Chapter 11 on John Bennett, Caterer to the Royals, I used the same sort of contract. At 6.00 p.m., we served an assortment of cold canapés and hot hors d'oeuvres. The guests seemed to enjoy the selection and we kept refilling the trays. All I could think of was what would happen if we ran out as they really went to town on the food and then I found out why. The guests thought this was all there was until they saw me and the staff replenish the table with silver chafers full of Beef Bourguignon and Egg Noodles with a mélange of fresh vegetables and a large bowl of Caesar Salad, minus the anchovies at the hostess's request. Well, they were gob smacked as they had never seen such a spread, including fresh hot bread rolls with butter and then, to go over the top, we served British Sherry Trifle for dessert with coffee and Sanka in silver pots, plus my own Petit Rours. This party was the talk of the town and brought us more

138

business from other hostesses wanting to have their own party with as much finesse.

Dick would arrive at my catering events without warning and I think he may have thought that I was having an affair with one of the guests as this seemed to be his insecurity, that every man was trying to get into my pants. At first I thought that he was there to see how the party was going and then as he presented the bill, he took all the bows for a successful party before leaving me and my crew to clean up. He told everyone that he was taking care of the books back at the Shoppe, but he was really working after hours on the booze. What books? I didn't realize until years later that there were no books although he was supposed to be a CPA and I left all finances to him. I found out much later that he did not even have the designation of CPA.

We were now the caterer of choice for the area, including the newly developed Sailfish Point that Mobile Oil owned. Mr. Raleigh Warner, president of Mobile Oil, used to have his pilot, Dave, call me when he was landing at the small airport in Stuart, to give his requests for food for his return flight to wherever he was headed. I took care of these requests and John would deliver the foods to the plane with all the necessary sides. The private plane was not huge, it had to land in foreign airports in such places as Arabia with small runways, but boy oh boy, it was a beauty. I particularly remember one trip when I was informed that Mr. Raleigh was to have some Arabian sheiks on board and therefore not to send any pork products for the trip, so I prepared meals without pork. But, I sent John with a special order of Mr. Raleigh's favorite food, my Chinese style baby back ribs, to deliver to the pilots cabin and a few wet towels, so Mr. Raleigh could excuse himself to check on how things were going with his pilot and at the same time have a good gnaw on the ribs, wipe the sauce from his face and hands, and saunter back to his guests for the rest of the meal. When Mr. Raleigh retired, I sent his wife the recipe for the Chinese style baby back ribs.

Dick talked to a couple who were interested in being part of the business and I believe they gave him cash. To this day, even though Ann is a great friend of mine, I have never discussed the arrangement because according to Ann and Ralph, they soon wanted out of the business and their investment returned. Of course, I was told an entirely different story from Dick, that they had in fact screwed us. I believed that for years and never had anything to do with Ann or Ralph until much later when I found out the truth. Ann went to work for my physician, Linda Kardos, as her office manager and still is to this day. I stop by the office to relive the good times we spent working together and we have a good laugh at all that transpired.

I catered the grand opening party of the Sailfish Point Clubhouse before there was any staff, except for the manager, a fellow Englishman. The party was for 250 local dignitaries and prospective buyers of very expensive model homes. We began by passing Cold Canapés with cocktails, and then a Buffet Dinner consisting of a classical salad with French Vinaigrette, which was placed at each place setting to allow the guests a free hand to hold their entrée plates. The Entrées were Contre Filet of Beef (carved to order), Seafood Newburg in a Vol au Vent Shell, Duchesse Potatoes, Tomato Farci and fresh made real Melba Toast in water lily napkins set on the guests' tables with butter shells.

On the dessert table I made a pastillage piece of the Cancer Society seal surrounded by pastillage orchids, all edible though no one dared touch them. Three silver tiered trays held Chocolate Mousse in Chocolate Shells, Petit Chocolate Eclairs, Petit Cherry Cheesecakes, and Swedish Gems. Coffee and Sanka was served from silver pots to each table.

I worked with Terri Monaghan of the Communication's Group to cater an island style cocktail party in front of the clubhouse for 150 guests to include a roast suckling pig, the likes of which no one had seen before unless they had been to Hawaii. All the help was dressed in colorful Hawaiian shirts with leis around their necks. I placed tiki lights around the area, an extra charge of course, and arranged for all the guests to have leis placed around their necks by exotic looking Hawaiian dancers, another special extra charge.

I stuffed the belly of the pig with lots of foil to fill out the sunken belly and a piece of wood in the mouth to keep it open for later to be replaced with an apple just about an hour before it finished roasting. I then jammed the oven door shut with a piece of board because the pig was bigger than I had planned for. We decorated the tables with hibiscus, banana leaves and exotic flowers to compliment the theme. This party was a cocktail type party, not a dinner buffet, but there was plenty of food as I had realized from past experience that these guests were out for the evening and even though it was a cocktail party, they tended to eat as if it was their dinner. So, I of course, adjusted my menus and prices to suit the situation. Cold tidbits (Cold Canapés) included Cherry Tomatoes Stuffed with Lomi (smoked salmon), Lychees Stuffed with Crystallized Ginger and Cream Cheese, Pipikaula (thin sliced sweet marinated dried beef), and Tropical Fruit Platter with Banana Liqueur Dip. Hot Pu Pus (hot finger foods) included Hawaiian-style Chicken Wings, Bangkok Pork Balls in Ginger Pineapple Sauce, Tahitian Pork Baby Back Ribs, Whole Filets Beef (sliced to order hot with condiments and small breads), Roasted Fresh Oysters from the grill, and Sliced Suckling Pig with Pineapple and Fresh Coconut Teriyaki Sauce.

Back in 1983, chicken wings were never used except for stock until suddenly they became popular and the wings which used to be given to me for nothing from the butcher were now in demand and sold for buffalo chicken wings. Another piece of meat called flank was so cheap that it was great for Chinese cooking but now it costs so much more. Flank steak was also used for London broil. When I first heard the term, I had never heard of it in England, but all meats tend to be called by different name in the U.S.

I was recruited by a nearby TV station in Fort Pierce, a few miles up US 1, to be on a show with Carolyn O'Neil and present a simple recipe in four minutes "live" once a week at noon. There was no time to attack anything unusual in four minutes and I had to take with me all the requirements for the show including mixers, toaster oven, two burner stove, knives, chopping board, oven gloves and dish wipes as the studio was not set up for a food show. Every time I went to the studio, I took Kledi with me and left John to look after the Bon Appétit Shoppe, to take care of our business and watch my live performance on TV. All the shows were a great success and I really enjoyed working with Carolyn. One day Carolyn called me and I thought it was about the next show but she told me that she was flying to Atlanta to meet Ted Turner, who was married to Jane Fonda, as he was recruiting for his new TV cable channel.

I had a live show that day without my friend but with a new young announcer left to hold the fort for this one time. He had never cooked in his life so I clued him in as to what I was doing and what was needed from him. I placed my butter in the pan on the stove and turned it on to melt the butter and to help the process along. I had my flour ready, my fish stock and sherry as I wanted the announcer to add the sherry when I asked him, along with the crab as I was making a Crabmeat with Sherry Casserole. Horrors upon horrors, the whole back section of the production stage had no electric but only just the front with the cameras and lights. *My God what do I do now?* I guess the pro in me kicked in as there was no way, or time, to do a thing about it so I kept on going, adding the flour and explaining to the viewer that due to the shortness of time, I must add the stock now and then my friend here will add the sherry. I handed the bottle of sherry to the young man and couldn't remember his name but I was lucky to remember mine at the time, telling him to put in a good swig, wishing I could have a swig myself, and then added the lump crabmeat. Now, I had a so-called hot finished dish in the toaster oven and with my oven gloves on I took out the clap cold crabmeat dish. As I placed it gently on the table, I told the young man to take a taste but explained, while kicking him under the table, that it was red hot and not to burn his mouth. Thank goodness he was a professional. When the show was over, I told the station manager that I had no electric and he said that it had not been obvious at all. I resolved there and then that I did not need this and in future would only do taped shows.

When I returned to the Shoppe, I checked with John and asked, "What did you think of the show?" He thought it was great, so I told him the story and he nearly died laughing. When I saw Carolyn a few weeks later, it was at an open house in Sailfish Point and I remember that I was busy poaching dim sum when she came up to me and said she had a proposition to make and took me outside to talk. She had been asked by Ted Turner to be the dietician for his new TV cable channel and she told him that I was the best person with the most food knowledge to compliment the programs and since we worked so well together, "How about it?" You can imagine this was quite an honor for me but I told her that I had to decline and gave the usual pat answer, there was the family business to run and my marriage to consider therefore not feasible (there was no way that Dick would let me do this alone). Of course, I was deeply upset inside, as the Turner Broadcasting Company had plans of expanding rapidly. Some time before, I turned down a nomination for Woman of the South, because Dick had not been included in the production. How stupid was that, but what else could I say? The food chef selected to work with Carolyn went on to write many cookbooks as well as make travel shows for Ted Turner. The name of the chef was Burt Wolf.

QUICK FOOD PROCESSOR BREAD
(makes 1 9 ¼" by 5 ¼" X 2 & ¾ inch)

1 pkg. dry yeast
1 tbsp. sugar
1 cup warm water
½ stick butter cut into pieces
3 cups unbleached all-purpose flour
1 tsp. salt

Stir yeast and sugar, please 1/3rd cup warm water in a bowl. Let stand till dissolved. Add butter. Using metal blade in place, add 2 cups flour, salt and yeast mixture. Process for a few seconds to mix. With machine still running, pour butter mixture through funnel in a steady stream. Process till mixed (20 seconds). Add remaining flour and process till smooth and elastic as shown (approximately 60 seconds). Flour hands and take dough out of mixer. If too sticky, sprinkle with more flour. Shape into a ball. Place in large oiled bowl and rotate ball to coat with oil. Cover bowl with plastic wrap and allow to rise in a warm place approximately 80 degrees till double in size (about 1 hour). Punch down as shown with fist and shape into loaf shape as shown. Place seam side down in greased loaf pan and loosely cover with plastic wrap after brushing top of loaf with oil Let rise till double in size (about 45 minutes). Bake middle oven 375 degrees for 35 to 40 minutes. Turn out on to cooling racks onto side to cool.

RAISIN BREAD

After dough has risen once, punch down and add 1 cup plumped raisins or currants to dough, then finish as above. OR roll into a rectangle about 7 by 20 inches brush with melted butter and sprinkle with raisins mixed with ½ tsp. ground mace and 2 tsps. grated fresh orange rind. Roll dough up tight and tuck ends under and place in pans as above to proof.

Chapter

13 BON APPETIT RESTAURANT

Since I was fourteen, my life has been involved in the food business, from the working man's café to fine dining establishments and hotels. And, to top it all off, I taught my trade to young students and to adults for their enjoyment. But the main thing that I enjoyed seeing was their eyes glow upon learning the art of cooking. I thought now that cooking school and catering would be it. But, boy oh boy, was I wrong.

Dick decided, along with Kledi, to expand the Shoppe and catering kitchen to include a restaurant. Their reasoning was that it was the best use for the adjacent vacant property. I mention Kledi, because whatever Dick said, she was under his influence and agreed as part owner of the property. I never knew exactly what part of the property she was part of; I was told it had nothing to do with me as I was not an owner. So here we were outfitting a fine dining restaurant, the only one in the area, and no competition for the style and décor that I would select. After construction, it would be sold completely furnished and ready to operate by an entrepreneur. Unfortunately, the idea was being discussed by Dick and his drinking friends and suddenly he became, Dick, the restaurant owner, with an ego that could not just build it and walk away, as he might have looked the town idiot.

The workers who constructed the cooking school, house and catering shop now got busy on the restaurant. John actually fell through the new rafters but was not hurt as he was my main man. I had trained my son and he was an excellent culinary graduate. John knew every waiter in town and became very fastidious about hiring the wait staff since he knew the requirements and this was to be Bon Appétit which he was to be affiliated with. Every waiter hired stayed with us as we were known as the best place to work financially. I did not hire females as waiters (back then) but as waiter helpers. These girls included my future daughter-in-law and also one of our Swedish waiter's wife, who had a knack for knowing what was needed by the customers and waiters. The restaurant was now finished and Dick was so proud over what he called his creation. Not only was the dining room top notch but the bathrooms, for both sexes, were elegant.

The Bon Appétit restaurant's ladies bathroom was decorated in Wedgewood blue with padded blue stools at the make-up tables with fine hand lotions, even my Tiffany perfume, but when the bottles vanished I did not replace them. One lady asked if her husband, a plumber could see into the ladies room. He was impressed with the men's room where over the sinks was a shelf holding lotions, soaps and cologne as well as fine paper towels with soap in a tray. All the wallpaper was washable, so the whole place smelled fresh with no stale grease or liquor throughout the restaurant.

I purchased different sets of chairs from estate sales but the dining room tables were restaurant size so they could fit together to make longer tables for parties and we had library-style folded doors to partition the main room from the Victorian room which could hold private parties like showers and small weddings. We became a favorite place for private functions such as pharmaceutical seminars for local doctors, where they could have a first class gourmet dinner with fine wine after a presentation. The room could only hold fifty but it was always fully booked with a waiting list for these affairs. The waiters knew how to flambé and carve a Chateaubriand for two, plus a real British mixed grill that really set the stage, usually enticing more customers to order these dishes.

The china, silver and silver cutlery was exactly the way that I wanted to present Bon Appétit. Every morning I had the kitchen to myself and as it was cool then, the cream and pastry was easy to handle and I loved the quiet so I could concentrate not only on the desserts but different appetizers that I was working on that needed my attention. I was recently looking through my recipes and photographs to see what I had done. For instance, there was the making of Gravlax, cured salmon my way for an appetizer. I had a regular home-style smoker which I used when smoking my own trout and lobster, and I made a type of puff pastry filled with lots of different savory fillings. I came up with making gourmet pizza on the grill which later other restaurants would do. I laminated my recipe cards so the crew could follow instructions. The chef and his wife worked with me but she seemed to know very little about the business and did not seem interested. Her husband, the chef, had no patience and shouted at everyone, including his poor wife, and never stayed true to the recipes that I had worked so hard at perfecting. When you go to a place where you previously enjoyed a certain dish and return with your mouth watering expecting to taste the same dish but it has changed does not make for happy customers. The chef and his wife left before the business suffered.

We found another chef, Dale, who was a culinary school graduate and after working with him for a few months I asked if he would like to obtain executive chef designation. Dale smiled and answered, "Yes, but how do I go about it since I work full time?" I explained that since I was a state of Florida teacher of culinary arts, he could study here and I would send his results to St. Augustine where he would receive his executive chef designation. A lot of chefs with little or no qualification at all use this title even though they are not executive chefs, as it looks good on business cards and menus.

When we were about ready to open the restaurant, we quietly invited some students of the cooking school and catering clients, requesting truthful comments to help get any kinks out. Everything went smoothly but I still did not want to advertise too fast. We arranged for two seating's on Fridays and

Saturdays, one at 6:00 p.m. and another at 9:00 p.m. as I hated to rush people through a relaxing fine dining experience.

My friend, Barbara Bell Matazuski, was food editor for the Stuart newspaper. She and I had judged many food competitions at local fairs, but Barbara did much more judging for the restaurant convention and show, where vendors came to the Orlando Convention Center once a year to show their wares. Many well-known TV chefs were there helping Barbara, who was the only female, to select who would win the Governor's Cup, all the pastillage, ice carving, and chocolate work competitions. As I said, Barbara was a food editor when she came to visit me at the restaurant for dinner with Fran, her husband, who was police chief of Sewell's Point. Word can get around quickly as to whether a place is good or bad so I did not want to advertise just yet, and thought it better to have a soft opening.

We were reservations only, so the pace was pretty much under control for me and I was able to sit down for a minute when Barbara and Fran arrived for dinner. She explained that being the food editor was getting to be too much, as she was already in the middle of writing one of her (food related) books. Barbara explained to the newspaper editor that she would be the food critique but there was no way to be incognito at Bon Appétit, and asked her editor to review me. So, she said, "Guess what, Pauline? You have been reviewed but I am not at liberty to say anymore." Of course, I understood but was on pins and needles while waiting for the review in the next Thursday paper. The review came out stating, "The food and setting was the finest in Florida, in our opinion," and when the other papers, the Miami Herald, the Palm Beach Post, the Indian River Pictorial and the Palm Beach Illustrated read the review, they all came to see what was going on and to see if the Stuart News was true. YES, YES, YES, ALL TRUE and I got top reviews from them all. Oh, happy day!

My son John had a commercial fishing license and on most days, he would leave early in the morning for his private (hush hush) spot. Other fishermen wanted to know where this place was but John was quick and careful to protect his special coordinates, or whatever they call them. He caught the best grouper, snapper and pompano available. I even made a book for him to show photographs of his catch. Most of the time, he had more fish than we could use so he would take them to the New England Fish Market. We bought lobsters and Florida stone crab claws, in season, from the market so it was a good relationship.

For readers outside of Florida, I must tell you that stone crab claws are delicious. Fishermen take only one claw, and then place the crab back in the sea so they can grow another claw and the next season, the crab has a new juicy claw to harvest and the cycle begins again with no loss to the crab. Joey's Stonecrab Restaurant in Miami only opens in crab season and is always packed with tourists for this sweet delicacy.

John brought in a super grouper one day and left it for the kitchen staff to handle, as he had to go home, shower and change into his waiter's outfit to begin work for the evening waiting on tables and selling wines to the diners. We had some diners who loved Beluga caviar, with condiments, and they usually had a bottle of Dom Perignon champagne to accompany it. John had a table of eight at 9:00 p.m., a very happy table I might add, and he explained about his fresh catch and one of the customers laughed, so John came into the kitchen and asked if the carcass was still in one piece and yes, it was, so he put it on a tray, placed the tray on a service cart and covered it with a tablecloth. He rolled the cart into the dining room, right next to the doubting Thomas and with a flourish like a matador; he whipped off the cloth and inquired of the customer if the grouper was fresh enough! The Godfather movie went through my mind as he did this except there was no horse's head, just a grouper carcass.

During this time, I developed bladder cancer and had surgery performed by Dr. Michael Lustgarten, and then BCG chemo. This occurred three times and the strange thing is when my primary physician, Dr. Linda Kardos, sent me to him the first time, he stated that he did not see any symptoms but when he performed an exam, he stated Dr. Kardos must be psychic.

In the summer after the Florida tourist season was over, the Orlando Convention Center held the Southeastern Food Service Convention to showcase all the latest food service products and hold competitions for such things as Pastillage work, (sugar pulling and the making of edible flowers that look real), chocolate work (and what creations they came up with). Of course, today you can see this on food channels but back then it was unique and the pastillage pieces that I made were jaw droppers. Barbara had been the only female judge and a pioneer in the department of judging, along with top chefs from the world and I was so honored to know her. The public, upon reading her food reviews were probably not aware of her credentials but if she judged someone's favorite restaurant too low thereby damning the review, it would play hell with her. The responses, real or made up by friends and owners, made Barbara laugh, saying it was good for newspaper sales.

I could not enter any competition (nor did I want to) at the Southeastern Food Convention but I was fascinated by the menu competition and just for kicks decided to enter our menus including the Sunset Gourmet Menu printed from my very old typewriter. Disney World, Universal Studios and many top name restaurants from all over the southeast were competing, and I mailed off my menus. Do you know I don't know if I told Dick that I had entered the competition? Dick, meanwhile wearing his owner badge, was busy tasting wines and John and I were checking out the hundreds of menus posted on folding screens looking for mine and wondering if they had been received in time. Finally, I inquired at the office and was promptly taken to my menus where they were not on the folding screens but in a

150

showcase with the first prize attached. My inexpensive menu won the prize. I must tell you that I had taken the time to explain each dish on the menu with the prices were written out (not numbers) giving it more class. Any dish that was low on calories or with lean meat, fully trimmed for the heart's sake, and different vegetarian dishes to entice vegetarians were all explained on the menu. Some dishes were written in French, if they were authentic French dishes, but with the full explanation in English, so no one felt intimidated by having to ask questions as to what it was. Now I had another plaque to hang in the restaurant hallway.

For quite a few years I catered private parties for Mr. Kiplinger, for his group and the trustees of Cornell University, so I knew them well. One of the writers wanted to write about the pros and cons of the restaurant business, so she got in touch with me, having met me numerous times at their corporate affairs, and asked to write an article using Bon Appétit as an example of the business. Dick became fully involved at such an opportunity and the article was nine pages long, with color photographs and quite the talk of the city. Customers who had their pictures taken signed a release to print them in the magazine and of course they enjoyed the experience to see themselves in a magazine that was published in just about every country, and in different languages.

I now felt too tired to do much more and to top it off Dick was diagnosed with prostate cancer so he sold the business to two of the younger chefs (family money) who immediately wanted to change the concept which did not work. Then, one of the young chefs was killed while riding his motorbike, so the luster went out of the place. Meanwhile, it was time to change my life, even though I was still married to Dick. I was tired of teaching and needed a change of pace. I turned down food writing or reviewing as I knew too many people and restaurants in the area so I began looking in the papers for positions in the food business (not management) knowing that something would come along that I could enjoy.

I had not made any moves to leave Dick at this time but looking back something was going on in my head because why was I thinking of just me at that time? My feelings were now of contempt for my husband but I still did not open my mouth, looking for maybe a future with him as an estate manager and me as his assistant, chef and executive housekeeper, where I would no doubt cover for him and bring in some money. The things that went through my mind at this time I cannot fathom and wonder if other women take so long to leave an abusive situation for fear of being a failure that their partners said they would be.

CHICKEN, APPLE, COGNAC AND CREAM PATE

The most requested recipe but never published before (except for cooking school students. Have 10 tablespoons butter at room temperature for later use. Ingredients: 3 tablespoons butter 1/2 cup chopped onion, 2 tablespoons chopped scallions, 1/2 cup chopped tart apples.

Sauté all the above to soften over moderate heat, do not brown. Place in blender. To the pan (do not wash pan) add 3 more tablespoons of butter and 1 pound chicken livers, 1 teaspoon lemon juice, and 1/4 cup brandy (flame the brandy if you prefer). Cook a few minutes to cook livers till brown. Place into blender with the above with 4 tablespoons heavy cream and salt and pepper to taste. DO NOT OVER SEASON. Make sure blender top is firmly on and then blend. Leave to cool a little then carefully lift off blender top and add the soft butter in pieces. Shake around to mix and stir (blender off if doing this). Taste and add more salt and pepper if needed. Cool then spread on crackers or place in a bowl surrounded with crackers and a spreader. I aspic glaze and decorate the top but a nice piece of parsley looks good and classy.

QUEEN VICTORIA'S FAVORITE
SPONGE CAKE FOR AFTERNOON TEA

All ingredients at room temperature, especially the eggs (whip better). Grease well 2 x 7 inch round pans (parchment on base and sides). Mix 3/4 cup fine sugar (I process regular sugar for a few minutes), 3/4 cup soft butter (not melted, just soft), and beat 3 room temperature eggs, beating them one at a time into butter mix. Sift in 1 1/2 cups fresh self raising flour (not old flour). Fold in the flour gently so as not to deflate the egg mixture. Divide between the two pans. Tap on the table to get out air bubbles. Bake 350 degrees. Check by piercing center with a toothpick, should be clean with no uncooked dough attached. Time approx. 20 to 30 minutes. Cool then split and fill with heavy whipped cream (or clotted Devon Cream usually served with scones) and strawberry or raspberry jam. Sprinkle powdered sugar on top using a sieve.

Chapter

14 C'EST SI BON PALM BEACH

I saw an advertisement in the Palm Beach Post Newspaper where a very famous gourmet shop called C'est Si Bon was looking for a person with gourmet food experience to work in their shop in Palm Beach, opposite a Publix grocery store with a different look than the usual Publix store. This store had a high hedge around it so it could not be seen from the road thus did not mar the appearance of the surrounding landscape. Many in Palm Beach hated the commercial aspect of having it in the town at all, especially as it brought people over the bridge from West Palm Beach into the community. This Publix had valet parking for limos and private cars and although store policy does not allow tipping at any of its stores, in Palm Beach it was normal to tip the bag person therefore the service people stay there until their dying days. It reminds me of back when the head concierge of fine hotels would sell his position upon retirement to the highest bidder.

I met with Aris and Arthur, the owners of C'est Si Bon and Patricia, Aris's wife, who was in charge of catering. Patricia's office and the main kitchens were in Lake Park where all foods for the shop were made fresh daily. As part of the interview, I presented my book of foods and photographs of my catered affairs in Stuart, only forty minutes away, and I was hired to begin the following Monday. My schedule was a six day work week (off on Sunday) and I tried to arrive early to help Aris and Arthur unload the truck of foods from Lake Park kitchen and decorate the platters to show their wonderful foods to the best visual advantage.

It was now the season in Palm Beach and since I knew most of the foods the shop stocked, including flash frozen foods so similar to mine, it did not take me too long to catch on. Being in what is referred to as Palm Beach 'proper', to differentiate it from West Palm Beach, the shop was well stocked with all grades of caviars, black and white truffles (not the sweet kind), Pinney's Smoked Salmon from Scotland, with the Queen's seal of approval on top, and as I said to the customers, "If it's good enough for the Queen, then it's good enough for me." We also had Pate de Foie Gras in a can, lots of pates from famous purveyors and the largest selection of ripe, ready to eat cheeses from all over the world, all in this small oasis of Palm Beach.

One of the shop's showcases that I was partial to was the showcase full of spreads and dips, not French onion soup style dips, but exotic spreads of lobster, crabmeat, shrimp and smoked salmon. No artificial krab as they call it or the washed out any old fish they call Surimi. How many times have you picked up lobster, shrimp or crabmeat spreads, turned over the package to read the ingredients and see no real seafood but the flavorless Surimi as the main item? Oh, the poor gullible public.

Well, at least C'est si Bon's ingredients were pure and most of the daily special foods were made on the premises. Eventually, I made the back room table into my kitchen with a toaster oven, mixer, piping bags with assorted tubes and pipe out these spreads into containers for the customer to take home for an impromptu cocktail party. Lots of assorted cold canapés were sent from the main kitchens but when we ran out of these I would get to work making cold canapés with many ingredients that I had available from the shop plus the tea sandwiches and caviar toast points. I don't ever remember having to say no to a customer for last minute requests. You will see how these ideas were put into use for a different venture.

I made many gift baskets at C'est si Bon. The gift giver would pick out a basket from the extensive array in the shop, we would walk around together selecting the contents appropriate for the occasion and then I would make the basket attractive to

155

fit the occasion, wrap it in shrink wrap with bows, etc. and hand deliver or mail it if out of the area.

Only in Palm Beach was an expression that came to mind when I was asked by a client to put together a seventy-fifth birthday gift basket (in doggy years). This dog apparently loved the better things in life, so here is what I placed in the basket. A fully cooked prime piece of tenderloin beef, Beluga 000 caviar, fresh blinis, Pinney's Smoked Salmon, cans of Pate de Foie Gras and after a quick trip to the doggy boutique for soft toys, no chew toys in case the poor darling had no teeth. The gift basket looked great and the gift giver was totally gob smacked. The basket was the hit of the party and a new trend was established for pet party baskets.

We were getting busier, so Aris and Arthur hired Daniel to help in the shop and decorate it for the holidays. Daniel has been the major domo, a term used for an estate manager by some of the estate owners which sounds so posh. His previous employer was Mrs. Woolworth-Donahue and apparently Daniel could do pretty much what he pleased, as the lady was rumored to be quite indisposed, having little knowledge as to what was happening around her. According to Daniel, she had the polished wood deck on her large boat replaced with a marble deck which, needless to say sank, with no hands on deck, thank goodness.

Another tale from the archives of the Woolworth-Donahue saga was that the house had numerous chandeliers, employing the full time services of someone to keep them clean and well lit without a single bulb left out of action. One day, Mrs. Woolworth-Donahue came screaming into the sitting room, looking for Daniel, as her twenty carat solitaire diamond was missing from her ring. Of course the staff was immediately under suspicion, so everyone was looking everywhere for the stone before the police were called. Eventually it was found in the chandelier workshop, as the chandelier worker had found it and thought it had dropped from one of the chandeliers. Daniel returned the diamond, redeeming himself and the staff. Now things were back to normal in this household or were they? Madam was broke and the estate was vacated for the next Palm Beach owner to refurnish and hire new staff.

So, in walked Daniel into C'est Si Bon, ready to decorate in his flamboyant manner, and to help take care of our customers with their food requests. Right away he got "Arthur's Goad," as they did not see eye to eye but the season was upon us and we had to get on with our work. I arrived early in the morning ready to help Aris with the truck and the foods from the kitchens and with Arthur's help; we were able to set up the foods, enticing customers to purchase. We see with our eyes first, then our sense of smell kicks in and our taste buds tell us that once again we have a great product to sell, but this was no hard sell for me as I knew the foods were full of the correct ingredients and no phony baloney. Daniel would get busy decorating the shop, then crouch down behind the dessert counter and munch on chocolate mousse, lemon mousse and any other goodies like Russian teacakes and real Palm Beach brownies that came on huge trays which I would then cut into portions and shrink wrap for the customers. The chocolate mousse was the mousse that Ivana Trump would purchase, which I mentioned back in Chapter 2.

I finally had my fill of Daniel's stealing and explained how it affected the profit of the shop and the employers who were paying him a paycheck. I kept my eye on him as often as I could but we were so busy that he got away with it for a while. Who were our customers? Well, such a great collection of "Who's Who" in Palm Beach. But, first, you must know that there are many great chefs in residence at many of the estates, and they knew that every week there would be a list of specials coming from our main kitchen. We offered different specials, cold and hot, and our list would be picked up by cooks from private homes, making C'Est Si Bon their own private kitchen where our foods would be passed off to their employers as their own. There were so many chefs being paid huge paychecks but were buying foods ready prepared from the shop and some had the audacity to ask me for information, which I did not wish to divulge, on other chef matters. Yes, I was a certified teacher and chef but when I worked for the shop, I was not about to give trade secrets away that would affect their business.

Mrs. Mollie Wilmot, an heiress of a large Boston department store, lived on the ocean with her swimming pool right next to the beach. One day, her maid woke her up much earlier than usual, since she normally slept later attending parties and celebrating all night long somewhere on the island, and told her that there was a huge tanker sitting slap bang in the middle of her pool. What did Mollie do? Well, she passed around glasses of champagne to all the crew, dressed in her usual short skirt and revealing top. Mollie was way past seventy but well taken care of by her plastic surgeon and she used any product that could keep her young at heart and body, though there was more emphasis on the look of the body. Mollie often had a boy toy with her when she shopped and sometimes he would have slicked back Rudolph Valentino style black hair and then another time, he would have blond curly hair. When people came into the shop, we were of course, professional and courteous with a smile, never showing our real feelings to the sometimes ridiculous styles of clothing and hair. Mollie was once asked by the local press as to who would be her next husband and she replied, "Darling, he has not yet been born."

Sir Robert Maxwell's daughter came into the shop and Aris introduced me to her, as her father and mine had been members of Parliament together, so we chatted for a while. I never mentioned her father's tragic suicide but instead talked about our fun filled childhood.

Mrs. Rollo Campbell often came to the shop and used our catering for their special charity affairs, raising money to make the local zoo a special place for the whole county. Since we were both British, we got to chatting and realized what a small world it is as years before our hotel in Bridlington had three acres of pristine lawn leading down to the promenade and to the sea. Dr. and Mrs. Campbell came by the hotel and asked if they could erect a large tent on the lawn to have a charity affair for proceeds to go to refurbishing the lighthouse in honor of their late sister Kay Kendall, who had been married to Rex Harrison (the famous actor who played Professor Higgins in *My Fair Lady and Dr. Doolittle* in another movie.

Most Americans did not realize Kay Kendall was queen of the British screen and stage. She was extremely great at comedy and everyone loved her. She passed away from cancer with her loving husband, Rex Harrison by her side. Mrs. Rollo Campbell now lives on Jupiter Island away from the heavy social scene but in a very exclusive area, also where Celine Dion, as well as Tiger Woods have homes. The residents are very low key but have the highest number of millionaires in the area, including Palm Beach. President Bill Clinton fell while visiting a friend, Gregg Norman (the golfer) and my son was hustled to the home to take control before the press got wind and blew the whole scene into something big.

Lilly Pulitzer enjoyed doing her own cooking, working in bare feet and dressed in one of her famous shifts that took the world by storm and still does today. I have two of these originals packed away as they do not fit anymore and are collectables. Every week Lily she would pick up food she needed to create special dinners frequently held at her home. I knew Lilly from Voisin, when I worked alongside her brother, who was guest host, so I was invited to her home to dinner; not to work but as a guest.

Another customer at the shop was a Broadway show producer who came in frequently along with her butler, manager, bodyguard and most faithful servant, but more on her in later chapters.

Jill was a fellow English girl married to an American businessman and she had triplets who were dressed as if ready for a party; they held their tiny purses and wore gloves as if in training for being a debutant. Jill's mother arrived from England to help with the children but very sadly Jill died leaving her young children without a mother and there became quite a battle with her husband's estate lawyers for him to take charge of the children.

Another good customer would order a whole cooked turkey breast for her dogs every week. As explained in early chapters, Donald Trump's wife would shop at the store, even though she had all the chefs and help to do what she needed but when it came to chocolate mousse and other special goodies, she came to our shop. Stephanie Wrightsman was and still is one of our good customers and an heir to one of the world's largest oil companies.

My job at C'est Si Bon was seasonal but the years that I worked there were the happiest, as I was working away from Dick, although my paycheck was handed over to Dick who would regularly telephone the shop to check if I had shown up for work, and when I left. Working there gave me an idea to make videos showing food store or deli owners how to add take-out catering to their business. Dick thought this was a great idea, as I would be doing all the work and he could take credit for it and Aris and Arthur would supply all the foods and trays needed for the project. Remember, there were no food videos of any kind at that time so it was a gamble, but I was ready.

Chapter

15 THE VIDEOS AND LIFE CHANGES

As mentioned in the last chapter, I had a brainstorm which kept me busy after the season at C'est Si Bon. I knew there was a market for teaching videos that deli and gourmet shops could utilize, no extra equipment or special help would have to be employed like chefs (the largest payroll expense), allowing owners to make more money with the use of these instructional videos and I also offered recipes to accompany the videos, for a very inexpensive fee. There was no such animal as the internet or computer, as everything was still done by typewriter. I bought whatever supplies were needed from C'est Si Bon, all the foods and take out trays when I was ready to begin filming videos.

My son, John, helped get the foods together and equipment for the film shoot and I had arranged for Peter Gorman, a great photographer in Stuart, to handle the photograph for the cover. Now, I had to work on this project in a hurry to keep expenses to a minimum. I made a call to Atlantic Video in Jacksonville, the closest video company for the shoot. Remember there was not a market for this sort of video and wedding videos were their bread and butter, and I was a novice at this project as much as they were. They were convinced that these two videos that I had planned would take at least three days but I had to do them in one day as the food that I had brought would perish in the heat of the film lamps, destroying the food in the one day. I had learned well from my experiences earlier with live TV and as money was so tight, I did not need any extra expenses. Dick contributed to the making of the videos by arranging to rent a truck to transport the food and equipment to Jacksonville.

The only difference between catering and this venture was that we had to hire outside help for the catering but this time it was up to John and I and Dick was following behind in his Lincoln. The day before we left for the video shoot, John and I took huge ice chests to C'est Si Bon, picked up the food, take out trays and miscellaneous items that I needed and headed back to Stuart to pick up the rest of the food, cutting boards, knives, wipes, even 409 cleanser, as we had no idea what we might need. Yes, band aids and plastic gloves, too. I actually cut my finger cutting the aluminum foil at the very beginning of the shoot.

We had the use of a small back room to do our videos and John knew exactly what I needed as he and I had rehearsed. I was concerned that it had to be perfect the first time before the foods disintegrated with the heat of the studio lights. The guys doing the filming did not expect me to finish two fifty minute videos that day, but little did they know at that time, that the food I had ready for the filming was just enough for a one time shoot.

It was bad enough that I was in a tizzy with Dick trying to control the whole thing with the film company, and me trying to get the food ready for the show was quite stressful, but I had to do it. No turning back now with *PROFITABLE CATERING MADE EASY volumes 1 and 2* ready to film.

The first video filmed me making party trays for an Exotic Tropical Fruit Platter with Orange Liqueur Dip and a Garden Vegetable Crudite Tray with a Crudite Spring Green Basket. Recipes for dips to accompany the trays included Curry Dip (recipe with this chapter), Dilly Dill Dip, Spinach Dip and Blue Cheese Dip, Whole Bries with Sugar Frosted Grapes, and assorted party spreads and pate trays. All were beautifully garnished with everything made from scratch.

As I started the first video, I cut my finger cutting foil and knew I had to start again as I thought the filmmakers were thinking to themselves that they had a real amateur here and were counting the dollars that this would cost us. Stressed and in a hurry, I had a quiet talk to myself saying, "Pauline, this is now or never," so forward I went pulling myself together. I finished the rest of the video all in one take. Now, I was ready to tackle the second video.

I went full steam ahead with the second video, creating elegant Canapés on a Bread Base as well as Pate, Shrimp, Salami Horns Farci, Smoked Salmon, and making Bread Croustades. I also showed how to utilize frozen commercial puff pastry to make Garlic Sausage en Croute, Goat Cheese Stuffed with Mushrooms, tomatoes and shallots ready to bake ahead, along with Brie Stuffed with Sundried Tomatoes and Ham. Nobody had prepared stuffed brie, etc. at this time. And, by the way, I prepared stuffed brie in puff pastry for the mother of the President of the United States for one of her parties in her home on Jupiter Island. I also showed sauces, pastry savory fillings, chutneys, and dips to utilize with these dishes. Red Pepper Hummus was a first at that time and now you can find regular hummus in any deli or grocery store. Recipe for easy Red Pepper Hummus is included with this video chapter.

So, we created two fifty-minute videos all in one day. The Jacksonville Company was astounded as they had not thought that it was possible but John and I did. Even Dick could not find fault with me this time. Later, back in Stuart, we recreated all the foods for the video covers, and prepared and copied recipes to go along with the videos when they arrived ready to sell. As I said, to my knowledge, nobody had done this before so now I had a product to sell at the next Florida restaurant show in Orlando, at the same place where I had won first prize for restaurant menus a few years before.

My sister, Ann, made skirts to cover the tables that I would use from the rental store including TV monitors to show the videos, and two smaller tables on which to place the videos while showing both videos at the same time. I displayed my credentials, diplomas and degrees to show my expertise and gave out brochures to people interested. On the first day, I sold quite a few, then more the next day and with promise for more sales. Chef culinary colleges also decided to order quite a few of the video combinations, which we shipped later from Stuart.

Upon returning to Stuart, I got busy preparing orders ready for shipment as I had to pack and ship alone since John was now employed as a restaurant manager for the Marriott Hotel in Palm Beach Gardens. Dick had not paid John for his time and work with me on this project, so with John's knowledge and experience, he was able to get this position with no problems. Now things were becoming even more unbearable around Dick. I kept a low profile, going out on video business to the library where I was able to go through college and university reference books to find prospective customers, writing their names and addresses down to solicit video orders. It so happened on this particular day at the library, it was actually our wedding anniversary but I feigned a stomach problem. It was also the same day that I finally saw the light after seeing a small book called *The Emotionally Abused Woman* at the library and knew that I had to get away as I explained long ago in the introduction of this book. Now, my life would change and my future was not with Dick.

RED PEPPER HUMMUS

Process 2 large chopped garlic cloves
1 – 15 oz. drained can chickpeas (garbanza beans)
½ cup Tahini (Sesame seed paste)
¼ cup lemon juice
½ cup roasted red peppers (drain well if using the jar)
Chop all fine in processor. Scrape down. Add salt and pepper
to taste.

CURRY DIP

(Excellent shelf-life in refrigerator). Mix together in a bowl:
2 ½ cups mayonnaise
1 cup tomato ketchup
2 ½ tbsp. curry powder
¼ cup grated onion
2 ½ tbsp. Worcestershire Sauce
1 ¼ tsp. Hot Tabasco

Chapter

16 A PRIVATE CHEF IN PALM BEACH

When my mother visited Dick and me in Stuart (by the way she never liked him and said that he was too full of himself), she put together a photo album of my life, copying my degrees, diplomas, awards, and photographs. Was she psychic, or what? Because later on, this became my best selling tool along with my resume and letters of reference, showcasing my multi-faceted talent to future employers.

I was ready to change my life with the help of an employment agency, resume, letters of reference and with my now deceased, dear mother's book. My son, John, drove me to the agency where I had made an appointment with Bernice and Lynne, to file the necessary paperwork they needed, including my resume. I was instructed to go to a medical facility, tested for alcohol and drugs, and returned A-1. When I went to the employment agency, I wore a black business suit with Ferragamo shoes bought at an upscale consignment shop, I believe they were all of ten dollars, and I, of course, had my briefcase. I also carried an old identity card from the Palm Beach Police Department which I had obtained in the early 1970's. In those days you had to show this card in order to work in Palm Beach. It is no longer required because it would be considered discrimination, but nevertheless, I still have it. Background checks were still required because you were dealing with millionaires and billionaires, CEO's of the top Fortune 500 and old Palm Beach money.

In short time, Bernice called me about a position that no one could handle, the owner had already hired and fired two couples. I interviewed for the position of live-in chef, which included a beautifully, appointed apartment. It even included a safe for my jewelry and special papers. I might mention that it was *Above Stairs* (above the garage), not *Below Stairs*. The lady of the house and her husband had hired and fired two other couples before me. They were quite particular as they wanted to have a formal European service in their home and apparently the other people were not up to their standards.

On the day of the interview, after Bernice and Lynne both assured me that I was the one that could fill this chef's position; my son dropped me off close to the Everglades Club and waited patiently while I went for the interview. The beautiful gated driveway and zoysia grass planted in between the flagstones extended all the way back to the house. Outside the kitchen there were bananas and pineapples growing. I rang the front doorbell of this gorgeous gothic style home and the gentleman himself answered the door. No butler. He took me into the sitting room and called for his wife to come downstairs to interview me. The lady of the house was followed by two beautiful, well- behaved Dachshunds named Monty and Carlo (named after Monte Carlo).

When I first saw Mrs. Gilmour I thought she looked like a china doll, immaculate, with a great welcoming smile. A fabulous couple, a May/December marriage, and they had been married for quite a few years, I think, twenty years or so. Mrs. Gilmour showed me the kitchen and it was gorgeous. They seemed impressed with my resume and my book, but they'd never tasted my food, so they asked me to cook and serve dinner for them the following evening. The menu discussed was Lobster Ravioli with a Cognac Shrimp Sauce as an Appetizer, Roast Duckling with a Peach Liquor Sauce, Singapore Rice and Petites Poise a la Française for the Entrée with a Treacle Tart served with Clotted Cream for dessert. No coffee, just wine. All the recipes were mine, except the English Treacle Tart, which had grated apple in it and I had never prepared this before (my recipe included). The dinner was a great success and they noted that I had used full French silver service and the correct wine service. Mr. Gilmour thought everything was just great but didn't think the tart was what he remembered as a child. I resolved to use my own recipe in the future, which I did, with great comments from their guests.

The house was a 1926 home, designed by Marion Sims Wyeth. It was refurbished with the help of Mrs. Gilmour, who had studied at the prestigious School of Interior Design, it looked gorgeous. I must say that this house was the nicest house that I was to work in. It was more cottage like, having only three bedrooms as well as the staff quarters above the garage. The dining room was very British, with English hounds and horse pictures on the wall. The dining room table was in the center of the room and it was round with English claw-foot style and English regency chairs, each one different. The set also included a buffet service. The house was full of antiques, spanning over 2,000 years. My main forte was, of course, the kitchen, with walk-in refrigerator, all commercial appliances and the whole countertop was covered in azure lapis marble. Mr. Gilmour had a custom built, temperature controlled wine cellar and Mrs. Gilmour often laughingly stated her laundry room space was cut in half to accommodate this walk-in wine cellar.

I was offered the position. Mrs. Gilmour took me into the garage and opened a door leading upstairs to what was to be my home, including a safe in the clothes closet, my own iron and ironing board plus a fully equipped kitchen, a beautiful living room, bedroom and bathroom. All was tastefully decorated including towels and linens, a TV and private telephone. The furnishings were actually from their apartment up north and the paintings displayed on the wall came from Mr. Gilmour's sister, a very talented artist who spent some time in the home during the season.

I got settled in but was still driving the old clunker of a car and since it was only in Dick's name, my boys decided I should get a new leased car. So, I leased a Mitsubishi and with my son John's help, we took the old clunker to a parking lot and my son called Dick to come pick it up. When I returned to work, I told Mrs. Gilmour that I had a new car and she said, "Let's go and kick the tires for good luck."

So there I was, a downstairs staff member living in the upstairs and the day that I started was my birthday. Mrs. Gilmour wanted to get her house in order for the season. Luckily, they'd hired a very handsome couple, he had worked for the builder who had refurbished the house and his lovely wife, who had previously worked in a laundry, spoke no English. Their names were Nelson and Monika. Mrs. Gilmour taught Monika housekeeping and between the two of us, we tutored them in the intricacies of setting the formal dining table for private luncheons and dinner parties, full French service and breakfast tray service. Since the Gilmour's had breakfast in bed every morning, Nelson and Monika became very proficient and I was proud of my part in this venture. To this day they are still there.

I would get up pretty early in the morning and quietly let the dogs out. They would follow me outside for their short and sweet morning ritual. When we returned inside, I set up the breakfast trays with all the silver needed and always with a vase of small flowers. Every morning without fail, Mrs. Gilmour would call downstairs on the phone to tell me that as soon as the staff arrived, would I please send up the breakfast trays. With breakfast trays, the staff would also take up the Shiny Sheet (the local Palm Beach newspaper) and the dogs. Now, with my list in hand and the money that Mrs. Gilmour always gave me each week for household expenses (for which I kept careful particulars) accounting for every penny, I would go to the local market, Publix. As mentioned in an earlier chapter, the Palm Beach Publix was different from the others in the Florida chain. This one had a high hedge around it so that it could not be seen; otherwise they would not have allowed it to be in Palm Beach and this market had valet parking. You could drive your car up, have it parked for you, and then when you came out with your groceries, you would wait in the valet area while they brought the car and loaded the groceries for you, but I never utilized this particular service. All the better foods such as caviar, grand dame champagne, and other goodies were available at this store.

On Saturdays, there was a greenmarket in West Palm Beach and I would go there to purchase all the fresh produce and herbs, even flowers. There were orchids, food available and demonstrations by local chefs. Live music played and dogs strolled on leashes, it was a very happy place to go. For the rest of my shopping, I would go to my friend's shop, C'est Si Bon, where I had worked previously, across the street from Publix. Here I purchased such goodies as Scottish Smoked Salmon, Truffle Oil, Pate de Fois Gras and fresh French bread. Now, as we Brits would say, "We're off and running."

Mr. and Mrs. Gilmour would have intimate parties for lunch or dinner and Mrs. Gilmour sometimes had friends in for afternoon tea. The dinner menus would often consist of some British foods like Roast Beef and Yorkshire Pudding plus something French such as Grand Marnier Soufflé which was served individually. Mr. Gilmour was so happy with the soufflés that he ordered special silver containers for them so that when the soufflés came out of the oven, I placed them in the containers, setting them on white linen napkins shaped like a water lily and then upon a dessert plate. They were then taken into the dining room with the Crème Anglaise.

Mrs. Gilmour would sit in the kitchen with me to plan the weekly menus. This included breakfast menus, any special luncheon or dinner menus, and the parties for that week. There were wonderful parties for eight people and a fitting number for the beautiful round table in the dining room. Conversation was so much easier when you had a round table. Dinner guests included prime ministers, presidents, lords and ladies and other foreign dignitaries. Guests of the Gilmour's also included a favorite author from my home county of Yorkshire, Barbara

Taylor Bradford, and a star from yester years, Arlene L looked fabulous just like I remembered her. Mrs. L would bring them into the kitchen to meet me, as she brought her guests into the kitchen to show off a wondeful clean and well appointed show place. The author was born in Leeds where I, too, was born so we had much to talk about. We spoke in our Yorkshire dialect which nobody understood, but it was rather fun. We would say to a perplexed audience, "put twood int hole" (put the wood in the hole, meaning, close the door. Simple, yes?

I needed to get my divorce and sanity back so I went with my attorney to the courthouse where Dick immediately grabbed my attorney's sleeve and started to tell her that I had bladder cancer which kept returning and I should remain with him until all the health and tax problems were solved. He thought that we had come just for a consultation with the Judge. My attorney looked at me and said that she knew I no longer had that cancer and that he had managed to spend all my hard earned money. My attorney asked me if I wanted a divorce today and, I said, "Yes," so she approached the judge and explained the urgency. Since there were no assets asked for in the divorce, the judge gave me a divorce and legally gave me back my maiden name of Pauline Tiffany. We ran out of there hell bent for election before Dick realized what had happened. It would take me quite a while to stop looking over my shoulder to see if he was following me.

I made English Eccles cakes and froze them ready. The cakes were more like a cookie and named after the town of Eccles but had been outlawed by the Puritans due to their exotic spices. The town found a way to get around the problem saying, "Here is to the Father, Son and Holy Ghost,'' making three slits across the pastry which convinced the Puritan church that these pastries were blessed and the bakers were back in business. I made and baked these treats fresh for guests to take home for their enjoyment, including Barbara Taylor Bradford, Arlene Dahl and many other prominent guests (recipe included).

Mr. and Mrs. Gilmour were very active playing golf and tennis at the Everglades Club so I would take the two dogs for walks on their leashes, side by side down Worth Avenue in Palm Beach. The merchants loved dogs and all were welcome in the stores as long as they were well behaved. I would take them to the doggie bar; no, not a bar where you can get alcohol but this was strictly for dogs. It was outside on Worth Avenue and there was water coming out of a fountain for all Palm Beach pooches, at ground level so all doggies could partake of liquid refreshment. Only in Palm Beach would you see this!

Now it was the end of the first season and the Gilmour's with their Louis Vuitton luggage packed, and the doggies with their Louis Vuitton crates, each with their own seat on the Concord, were off to Paris for the summer, and thinking of side trips, including Great Britain and the island of Wakaya which the Gilmours owned and eventually bottled the water for export called Fiji Water. I had been thinking of taking it easy during the summer, off season, except that I received a phone call to fill another position during the summer, for a famous rock and roll star of which I shall tell you in a later chapter.

The Gilmour house was now shuttered and ready for hurricane season. Nelson and Monika stayed to keep the home ready, including the gorgeous gardens, with orchids from the season transferred and tied to the trees to take root. After the summer season in Europe was finished, Mr. and Mrs. Gilmour returned with the dogs, to Palm Beach. Mrs. Gilmour wrote to me ahead of time to let me know what they would need for the first week so I was ready with fresh stocks, as always made from scratch, with as much preparation as possible for both the kitchen and the butler's pantry.

The butler's pantry is where all the fine china, Lalique crystal and other fine stemware were kept. Even the silver platters were finely polished with help from the staff. The house had two dishwashers; both in the kitchen, but all the fine china, crystal and silver were hand washed in the butler's pantry. We laid out dish towels so we would have no damaged glassware or china and less noise away from the dining room.

Mrs. Gilmour played tennis and golf, and as usual, impeccably dressed. She always looked so elegant. She used to say to me, "You know Pauline, just because Palm Beach residents are wealthy, they're not all ladies and gentlemen with good manners," and she was certainly right. I remember one evening the Gilmour's had guests for dinner and there was a certain lady that I later told Mrs. Gilmour about, who came into the kitchen and offered me a job working for her. Of course, this was not to be tolerated and Mrs. Gilmour said, "She'll never come to my home again. Imagine trying to steal my staff."

Mr. Gilmour had a heart problem and had to go for an operation in his homeland of Canada and when they returned to Palm Beach, Mrs. Gilmour acted as his nurse. I had to refine all of the recipes and make them fat free. In fact, I could make Yorkshire Pudding with egg whites. When there were guests coming for dinner, I made a special look-like Grand Marnier Soufflé, fat free for him so it was not obvious to his guests. I adopted Dr. Dean Ornish's program, tweaking the recipes a little bit because I was working for a gourmet, but keeping true to concept. I know it helped them both. Mr. Gilmour soon recuperated but we kept to the diet, except of course when they were invited to parties at someone else's house.

A dinner party in which the Gilmour's had been invited to ended in a fiasco and made the Palm Beach Shiny Sheet newspaper, but I got the scoop first hand. The guests had just sat down for dinner, the butler brought in the soup tureen and the lady of the house ladled the soup onto soup plates. The butler then served each guest and after the guests finished their soup, the hostess waited for the next course. She kept pressing the bell under the table which rang in the kitchen but was not heard in the dining room. Many Palm Beach homes have this kind of service bell including the Gilmour's' as it allowed privacy without staff present. It was a wireless bell from the dining room to the kitchen, so the butler went to the kitchen. He was a huge man and when he returned to the dining room, he bowed down quietly whispering to the hostess who immediately excused herself and went into the kitchen. In the center of the kitchen table was the soup tureen with a note attached which said that all the staff had quit because nobody could stand working for her and, adding insult to injury, they also mentioned that one of them had peed in the soup. It was pea soup, I presume! The dinner finished abruptly and Mr. and Mrs. Gilmour returned home early and related the story to me. The story soon appeared in the Shiny Sheet newspaper so it was not exactly a state secret as apparently someone had leaked the story. I wonder if it was one of her disgruntled staff.

The Palm Beach Daily was called the Shiny Sheet because of the high quality paper they used. The ink would not come off onto the hands or the sheets while reading the paper in bed or on the table linens in the breakfast room. In the days before this special paper was used, the butler or laundress would iron the paper to set the ink and get out the creases. I was taught this task while in college along with other ironing classes. Father would always let me starch, using liquid starch, and iron his shirts because he said that no one could do this as good as me.

I really enjoyed my time working for Mr. and Mrs. Gilmour. Before they left for Paris, the staff and I were nicely told that the French couple who had taken care of their Paris home had quit and they had hired a new French couple to travel with them in the USA and Europe. We were urged to train this couple (who were to take our jobs) and they were supposed to be professionals. We had only three days to work with them because Mr. and Mrs. Gilmour were about to leave for Paris to open their home there. So we did the best we could. The woman was the cook and her husband was the butler and chauffeur.

When the French couple arrived, we soon realized that we had to teach them everything. They did not know how to set a table and had no idea how to set a breakfast tray. The butler and chauffeur stayed on the phone in the kitchen talking to relatives in Paris and did next to nothing except serve. The cook was messy and stuck her fingers in the food for tasting. I always had a dish with teaspoons in water sitting at the side of my station so that I could taste the food and never touched my hair or my face while in the kitchen. We had all religiously washed our hands over and over and as Mum used to say, "Cleanliness is next to Godliness!" The cook said that she would prepare us a meal whereupon my co-workers looked at me without knowing what to say but I told a white lie and said, "Oh, I always prepare our meals in my apartment." Of course, I never did as we ate our meals downstairs in the kitchen. So, since I had very little food in my own apartment, Nelson snuck out of the house through the garage to buy some sandwiches. We could not say anything to our employers because they had to have this help to open their home in Paris and there was absolutely no time to change anything. So the French couple left for Paris.

Now, their day of reckoning arrived and Mrs. Gilmour asked about their progress so with my colleagues in tow I told her the truth. She replied, "Oh my, we have just hired the most expensive dog sitters in history as we will never eat a thing in our Paris home." Even though we had all been terminated, she asked my co-workers to stay as I had already made other plans.

Mr. Gilmour hired a young chef, who had been featured in one of the food magazines, to cook for them and their guests. Apparently upon his arrival, he started to order more appliances as if he was outfitting a restaurant instead of a private home. I also heard that he bought many new spices and other foods which caught his fancy, had the nerve to ask Mrs. Gilmour if he could call her by her first name, and inquired if his girlfriend could visit him in his apartment, which of course he was told, "NO."

After working the first season for Mr. and Mrs. Gilmour, while they were in Paris as I mentioned earlier, it was to be vacation time for me, but instead, I received a call from my friends at C'est si Bon, letting me know that an interior decorator was looking for a chef for three weeks for a famous star. After the interview, I realized who the star was and it turned out to be Rod Stewart who wanted an accomplished chef who could cook British food for his family. The children were normally fed by their nanny but not this time as I would cook fresh food for the little ones, not canned or frozen manufactured foods that apparently the nannies cooked.

ECCLES CAKES

Puff pastry sheet rolled thin. Hold.
In Saucepan, add 2 oz. butter and 3 tbsp. sugar. Melt and take off heat.
Add 4 oz. mixed raisins, currants, 2 tbsp. finely chopped candied peel
½ tsp. nutmeg
½ tsp allspice

Cut pastry into rounds, 3" cutters. Place a little mix into center.
Wet edges of pastry and draw edges into center to cover mix.
Press down. Place on lightly-floured board (flat top facing up) and roll out thin (fruit may show). Beat 1 egg white with a fork to break up. Brush egg on top, sprinkle with sugar. Place three slits on top to signify the Father, the Son, and the Holy Ghost.
Bake till slightly brown on a greased cookie sheet approximately 10-12 minutes at 350 degrees.

TREACLE TART

Filling:
2 cups English Golden Syrp or light molasses
2 ½ cup fresh white breadcrumbs
1 tsp. lemon juice
¼ tsp. ground ginger
Mix Together

Use piecrust pastry. Make a 9-10" pie or two dozen small muffin pan tarts. Prick slightly, add filling bake golden brown 350 degrees.

Chapter

17 ROD STEWART THE STAR

Rod Stewart had a very good looking home. So elegant, nothing loud and outlandish as one might expect from a rock star; he had exquisite taste. Superb furniture and antique pictures were sent from Sotheby's New York and London. While he and his family were in residence, I hired off-duty police officers. I also rented orchids from a local florist, short stays with full blooms and placed in the jardinières on tables and even the bathrooms. Then, when my employer and family departed, the orchids were picked up and replaced with fresh when they returned. Rod Stewart loved sports cars and he told me the reason he was in the music business was long ago to afford a sports car to pick-up chicks. He was married to the famous New Zealand model, Rachel Hunter, which was not his first marriage, and previously married to Alana Stewart, and the teenagers due at the house were from that marriage. Renee and Sean were the children with Rachel and Rod.

Before the family moved in, I received a letter from their male secretary in Los Angeles with requisites for their arrival. There was a British shop down south near Boynton Beach, I'd been there quite a few times, so I gave the owner a call and told her who I was working for and gave her the order. She said to me, "Oh, please, may I deliver?" and of course, I said yes because that saved me a trip.

The day the family arrived was a happy one. I received a call ahead of time from Alana Stewart, the mother of the teenage children soon due in from California, asking me to please take her credit cards from them and hold them. Sounds so typical of teenagers today, but what a strange first introduction to the family. Mr. Stewart's oldest daughter knew British food and asked me, "Can you do Bananas and Custard?" to which I replied, "Well, of course." She enthusiastically then said, "I want this for every single meal while I'm here!" (recipe included) Well, there were better things on the way that week; so of course, she didn't hold me to that request. Mr. Stewart used to say, "Why are we going out to dinner? We've got the best food in Palm Beach right here." It was such a nice compliment to me and so nice to feel appreciated. When he was around the house, he wore blue jeans and T-shirts which were more comfortable than getting dressed up to go out to dinner.

Palm Beach people are not star struck and I was used to stars, royalty and everything else so it didn't bother me as well. In fact, when I first started to work for him, Mr. Stewart asked me if I liked his music to which I replied that it was actually not my cup of tea and he laughed. He had a beautiful baby grand cream-colored Yamaha in the living room, same color as my piano which is a Yamaha too, but mine was not a baby grand. I can't say that I didn't play it but I certainly didn't play it when they were there. After all the only way to keep it in tune is to play it.

While I was living at the house, I was laughingly referred to as the woman who slept with Rod Stewart. Of course, I clarified this statement as I had a reputation to keep after all I was single now, having made the mistake of marrying not one, but two men of very little moral character.

Many of Mr. Stewart's friends and stars came to visit and I would prepare dinner for them. One famous star stopped by my room once, I was playing my piano and suddenly there was a knock on my door and there was Elton John. "Can I come in and tickle the ivories?" which in England means to play the piano. I said, "Of course, I would love you to." So he came in, I stopped playing because there was no way I would play his caliber of music and would have consequently been embarrassed.

Many guests dined with the Stewarts' and I provided home cooked meals made from scratch. Well, the three weeks turned into months, even though I'd made a commitment to return to my previous job. It was strange living in a star's home and keeping away paparazzi and fans. I even checked through the mail, separating business mail from fan letters, and oh, how they ranted on about how much they loved Rod, etc. One day, someone rang the doorbell with a delivery of a floral arrangement from what I thought was one of the local florists, then I realized that I'd been had. I put my foot in the door when she said, "I need to see Rod" and I said that I'd deliver the flowers or she could simply leave; she left the flowers and took off. Maybe she thought I was his dominating sister but as the door was closing, I heard cheers from the upstairs balcony where Mr. Stewart was letting me know that I had done a good job.

Mr. Stewart's family, including his brother, were down to earth people. I spoke quite a few times with them on the phone and one time, I received a phone call from his brother saying that their mother had died. Mr. and Mrs. Stewart were out and there was no way to get hold of him with the news as he did not carry a cell phone, so I had to wait until he came home to give him the news. His secretary in Los Angeles made plane reservations for his flight and I made sure that he had his green card for the trip. We were setting the dining table that evening just before he left and he said to me, "My mother had quite a voice and they tell me that she died singing."

I sometimes used to think that Mr. Stewart was spending more time in the kitchen talking to me than in the dining room with his family. When he was in the kitchen watching me cook, he would smell tempting aromas, roast leg of lamb or roast beef and Yorkshire pudding, and he would tell me, "Just a little nibble" and then steal a bite or two. If it was lamb, he would want some of my fresh mint sauce (recipe with this chapter) as I would never dream of serving mint jelly why that was sacrilegious! We had fresh mint sauce. Sometimes when I returned from shopping at the local stores, tour buses came by the house and being British, I had a "GB" sticker on the bumper of my car and they would stop and take photographs of me driving my car. They must have thought that I was somehow part of the family, and I, of course, just smiled.

One time, I went to C'est Si Bon to get Stilton and cheddar cheese, and guess who was there? It was the lady, and butler, that I talked about in the last chapter with the dinner party turned fiasco. When they left the shop they forgot a few of their purchases, so I told Aris, the shop owner that "I'm just a few doors away from them; I'll save you the trip and deliver it for you." So a call was made and they were told that their order would be delivered. I went to the service entrance of their home and rang the bell. The butler's voice came over the intercom and said a loud "Hello," and I replied, "I've got some food from C'est Si Bon," and he said "Come in," and opened the gate. I went to the kitchen door and handed him the food and he said, "I guess you need a tip, don't you," and I said, "What? I don't think so. I just happen to live a few doors away at the Stewart residence and since I was in C'est Si Bon at the same time that you were, I offered to drop your forgotten items off on my way home." Well, his attitude changed completely. He didn't know where to put himself. Here he was trying to give a tip to one of the star's family, or so he thought. He got one heck of a shock, which served him right for being so mean to people. I had heard stories of his taking advantage of female illegals in return for a job, room and board.

In the Stewart's residence upstairs, by taking the elevator or the steps, there was a theatre set up for the children to use. There was a karaoke machine, dressing rooms and wardrobe with plenty of clothes so they could entertain guests. They had their father's talent and I enjoyed watching them immensely from the backstage.

I received a check now and then from the main office but often had to use my own money for groceries. I did, however, receive a paycheck every week but ended up paying out my cash for the groceries. I asked Mrs. Stewart for grocery money but it was embarrassing when she said that she had no money, so I asked what I should do and she told me to stop buying food. I was instructed not to bother the star, as he was on tour around the east coast of Florida. He had a limousine pick him up, take him to the airport, fly to his venue by private jet and return to the house in Palm Beach. The main problem was a lack of cash, problems with his company not paying bills owed to several businesses, including a large bill that the main office in Los Angeles owed to the local decorator for thousands of dollars. Later, after I left, the decorator's outstanding bill resulted in a law suit and it was in the papers, and thoroughly enjoyed by the press worldwide.

There were three female employees flown in from California to handle the housekeeping and they called the Stewart's by their first names, though I would never dream of being this familiar with them or any other of my clients. It appeared to me that they took advantage of a free vacation and managed to do just enough work and just enough personal attention to the family when they were around.

Mrs. Stewart's sister, Jackie came to bask, not only in the hot sun, but in the glory of being part of the family. She and I, to put it very lightly, did not get along. Jackie was very demanding of special meals from me and refused to help in any way. For instance, I remember one lunch the family decided to eat at the Gazebo, not far from the beach but it was over sand and I was unable to use a cart to transport the food and set up the table. If Mr. Stewart had been there, he would have helped me but he was away on tour, so I asked Jackie to open the door and close it after I got through with the cart. Jackie refused and slammed the door in my face stating that I was the chef and server while the boss was away and the other staff was instructed not to help me.

One weekend, Mrs. Stewart and the nanny took the children to the water park in West Palm Beach. They enjoyed themselves and had fun without being recognized as Mr. Stewart was not with them. It was not easy to fool the public even when he wore baseball cap. That same day, Mr. Stewart and I were in the kitchen and he was sitting at the kitchen table making miniatures with matchsticks for his railway set in Los Angeles, and he commented that was his way to relax. I had just made us a cup of tea when there was a knock on the kitchen door. There was security at the front and the children were not at home, so Mr. Stewart followed behind me as I answered the door. There was a wet and bedraggled man in a swimsuit, apologizing for disturbing us but he had been walking along the beach and the tide came in and he had to get onto land. He saw the beach umbrellas and toys outside and figured there must be someone in residence (by now most homes in Palm Beach were shuttered for the summer) and asked if I could let him out the front gate. Mr. Stewart stood behind me, as if I was a bodyguard, and I told the man to follow me to the service exit. As he left, he said to me, "Is that who I think it is?" and I told him yes but to keep quiet or the police would be coming to see him for illegally entering private property. Mr. Stewart asked if I thought it was a truthful mistake and I told him that I believed it was, so there was no need to call the police.

The Stewart family kept coming and going for the next months and my time with them was coming to an end as Mr. and Mrs. Gilmour were due back for the winter season. Mrs. Gilmour had already sent me her foods list for their return and I was happy to be getting back to the Gilmour's house for our usual winter season. So, with all my bags packed and my piano already removed, I was ready to return to my old apartment.

My last day at the Stewart residence, Mr. Stewart arrived alone with the family due to arrive later. I mentioned that a beautiful old restored Bentley was in one of the garages and he asked if I needed anything from the store for the house so he could try out the car. I said that maybe some more milk from Publix but I assured him that he would not enjoy the experience in this busy store with all of its many customers. But he said, "Let's go. I shall be the chauffeur and you will sit in the back." Now, remember, this Publix had valet parking but Mr. Stewart was not about to let his new toy be parked by anyone but him. All the store managers came out to the center of the store seeing it was the first and probably the last time Rod Stewart would visit them. Shoppers stopped him and gave him pieces of paper for his autograph, which he signed with pleasure. I will never stop admiring him for the patience he had with fans, being stopped on the street with a smile and comment, "Good day mate." People did not ask him for an autograph when he was on Worth Avenue shopping with the family; no one bothered him as they realized and respected his privacy.

Most of the staff knew me at Publix since I shopped there most every day when the family was in residence. One of the Publix employees had had breast cancer and I told Mr. Stewart what a great fan she was and asked if she could meet him. Mr. Stewart asked her to come to the front of the counter, gave her a gentle hug, and signed his autograph on a piece of paper for her with a special message. He never carried photographs, as that was left to his staff in Los Angeles, because Palm Beach was for private relaxing where the rest of the world could pass by, most unaware of his home here.

Eventually we made it to the check-out counter where Mr. Stewart said to Marlene, a long time employee, that the price of groceries kept going up all the time and she was agreeing with him not knowing who he was and just kept on chatting with him. Of course, everyone in line realized who he was and enjoyed the interaction between customer and cashier.

After we left, the staff told her who he was. By the way, Mr. Stewart told me to tip the man that took the cart of food to the car. We were about to return to the house but he realized he had promised Renee some violets for her room and I begged him not to go back into Publix. The Publix in Palm Beach had lots of celebrities in their store but Rod Stewart was the type that they could talk to. Down the other street was a small flower shop that I had never been in before. Maggie May, the bulldog, named after Rod Stewart's hit song so many years before, met us with her owners. Mr. Stewart took some violets out of the sliding refrigerator door, then some daisies out and said to me, "Why don't we make an arrangement for the foyer?" I reminded him that I was to leave today but that I would, of course, help him and I also reminded him that the house was full of orchids. After he paid for the flowers, the owners said, "We sure can tell that this is your sister," to which he replied, "If she was my sister, she would not be leaving me today, would she?"

FRESH MINT SAUCE

Chop fine 1 cup fresh mint leaves. Hold.
In a saucepan, place:
 3 tbsp. sugar
4 tbsp malt or white vinegar

Cook to melt sugar only and take off stove. Add mint leaves.
Then refrigerate. Holds indefinitely. Great for any lamb dish,
even a teaspoon in cooked carrots or peas for flavor.

BANANAS AND CUSTARD

British Bird Eye custard powder is available in same grocery
store, or if not, here is an easy alternative.

1 ½ cups Milk
1 ½ tbsp. sugar
½ tsp. vanilla extract
Spot yellow food coloring if needed
2 tsp. cornstarch
3 large room-temperature egg yolks

In heavy-bottomed saucepan, place 2 teaspoons cornstarch with
2 tablespoons of the milk and mix till dissolved. Add the rest of
the milk and sugar. Cook over moderate heat, stirring until it
comes to a boil and thick. Place the yolks in a mixer and beat
for 20 seconds. Take a cup of the sauce and beat in as you pour.
Return this yolk mixture to the sauce and return to boil. Add
vanilla extract and spot of yellow food coloring if needed.
Remove from heat and use individual glass dishes or a bowl.
Place custard in bowl, then a layer of sliced bananas, custard,
bananas and finally topped with custard. Cool and serve.

Chapter

18 MR. HURBAUGH
THE PERFECT GENTLEMAN

My agent called me and said that she had a position with an older gentleman whose wife had died. Mr. Hurbaugh had Parkinson's disease, which was under control at the time, and he also suffered from macular degeneration. His family, especially his son had requested a man to take this position. My agent convinced Mr. Hurbaugh's daughter to at least see me, so I went to his weekend home on a golf course. He and his wife had originally lived in Palm Beach and had been involved as chairpersons on many balls for charities. But, following his wife's death, he sold the Palm Beach home and the house on the golf course now became his winter residence. Summers were spent in Rye, New York.

I went to his house and was greeted by his daughter, then taken to meet this gentleman and we had a good chat. Apparently all the male applicants spoke little English, no idea how to cook and could not communicate with Mr. Hurbaugh. We had a good 'natter' (talk) and I left my resume and letters of reference feeling that since I was not male, that I would not get a return call but I was wrong. The next day, his daughter called and asked me to come by the house and drive her father to the club for lunch with them. I guess it was to test my driving skills in his car.

At the club, people were naturally curious to see Mr. Hurbaugh, his daughter, and this other lady. After all, Mr. Hurbaugh had held his dead wife as the love of his life, which she was. Many members and his friends came over to the table and I loved what he said to these people when he introduced me as, "This is Mrs. Tiffany," and nothing more but the looks on their faces said it all. We often laughed later about this introduction, because we could see the grins on people's faces, whirling around to take another look. Mr. Hurbaugh had such a wonderful sense of humor. According to his daughter, he wanted me to be his estate manager and chef, and I had use of the Chrysler convertible, also the Lincoln, but I only used the town car when I was taking Mr. Hurbaugh out because he had claustrophobia and the town car was much more comfortable. He could no longer drive, so when I drove him, I talked a lot to keep his mind off of his claustrophobia. It worked, especially when we traveled. We were to make frequent stops to stretch our legs during our travels on the New Jersey Turnpike and I-95. Mr. Hurbaugh employed a driver in Jupiter and later when in Rye, New York, for the summer season.

After Thanksgiving, Mr. Hurbaugh flew down to Jupiter and was accompanied by his only son. Mr. Hurbaugh requested a simple meatloaf (recipe included), and left the rest of the menu to me. The house was ready for him, even his special roses, placed by his wife's photograph in his library which I ordered and had delivered for him every week. The dinner was a great success, including the way I set up the dining room table, as the son called family to tell them all about the great dinner. Mr. Hurbaugh was taking care of himself at this time but that soon would change. He had a housekeeper who vacuumed around the chairs, never moving them and even did her own family's laundry at Mr. Hurbaugh's house. But at this time, I decided to leave things alone as I did not want to upset Mr. Hurbaugh since he had a good life going for him at the moment and it wasn't until later that things changed.

Mr. Hurbaugh's son's partner was an Episcopalian minister of a church in New Jersey but unfortunately it became obvious the son was using his father's credit cards and had managed to spend quite a lot outfitting the Vicarage. In the past, when minister's had families at the Vicarage, they would use all of the upstairs rooms for bedrooms but this time two rooms were made into a revolving clothes closet, similar to what drycleaners have. They had many catered church functions but nobody really watched or realized how much money was spent, except the son, me and the secretary. I was very upset that his son used his father's cards to purchase cruise tickets for himself and the minister, using thousands of dollars to go on cruises leaving from Fort Lauderdale. The men sometimes stayed overnight at the house, not so much because of family love for Mr. Hurbaugh but because of his money. What a real shame. I had been given a credit card by Mr. Hurbaugh for supplies and kept close track of the activity but suddenly became aware that when the boys had been here, the son must have gone into my purse and taken the numbers off my credit card and was using them. He knew his father's social security number so it wasn't hard for him to get what he wanted. I could not keep this from my employer, since after all it was in his name and I felt responsible. I spoke to Mr. Hurbaugh's older daughter and she was not surprised as she had heard this same story before, even from her deceased mother. The secretary, Barbara, was hated by the son and I soon realized it was because she caught him in this kind of behavior so many times.

One morning, Mr. Hurbaugh received a package via UPS and because of his eyesight, I opened the package. There was a young boy on the cover of the video and he said, "I think this is an exercise video for one of the youngsters, what do you think?" and upon reading the back cover of the video, I realized it was pornographic. Apparently, Mr. Hurbaugh's son used his father's credit card and the package was sent to the credit card owner's address instead of the Vicarage. Mr. Hurbaugh's daughter called the video company and stopped all further orders, called the son and his lover, and gave them both a piece of her mind. Believe it or not, the Hurbaugh address was already on lists with other similar companies so I began checking and sorting the mail every day. (Just like I did when I worked for Rod Stewart, but this time, for entirely different reasons). Every time the son came to the house, I hid his father's credit cards and mine. I had

189

a couple of Louis Vuitton luggage pieces that suddenly went missing during the son's visits. These pieces were for men or women, including the recorder valued alone at $1,200 but I never said a thing, I did not want to distress Mr. Hurbaugh.

Mr. Hurbaugh had no idea about his son's sexual preference and naive about these matters. His daughter laughingly said to me one day that she had no idea as to how she was born as her father was not into sex. Mr. Hurbaugh told me that he thought his son had a serious girlfriend, as he was always buying her expensive gifts. Well, it turns out that his son would arrive with a girl and then along came the minister with another girl. Apparently both girls were lesbians and since the bedrooms were upstairs with long balconies, private bathrooms, as well as a nursery, no one downstairs in the master bedroom suite had any inclination as to what was happening.

Poor Mrs. Hurbaugh apparently knew the score, since before her death, their son had sent formal announcements to his marriage with the minister to all of their friends and business associates of the family. What a shock!

The winter season arrived with parties at the Everglades Club and lots of other private clubs in Palm Beach, which were mainly black tie events. At the beginning, Mr. Hurbaugh would accompany one of his deceased friend's wife and take her to the balls. I did not participate so instead I would go to Testas Restaurant, a landmark in Palm Beach, known especially for their strawberry pie. I always ordered their great crab cakes with the lobster sauce, then drive back and pick up Mr. Hurbaugh and his guest. There I was sitting at the Everglades Club with the other drivers who were all chauffeurs in uniform, except me. After a couple of these engagements, Mr. Hurbaugh told me the ladies were worried about my intentions and he explained that I was his estate manager and his chef with no other purpose and that was it, period.

Most people, except Mr. Hurbaugh's closest family and friends, could not possibly understand that he had had only one love all of his life and needed no further attention. So, Mr. Hurbaugh requested that in the future, I was to come with him to his social obligations. I wore elegant clothing and had a mink stole and mink coat, thank goodness for Palm Beach consignment shops. The season passed and his driver, Joe, from New York came to pick up the car which I had filled with clothes for both of us whereupon on arrival, Joe would get the maid to unpack the clothes and place my things in my suite. Mr. Hurbaugh's driver in Jupiter took us to the West Palm Beach airport for New York. I had my hands free, having sent the luggage ahead, so that I could help Mr. Hurbaugh.

We arrived at the club where Mr. Hurbaugh had a large apartment in which he and Mrs. Hurbaugh had lived. Previously, they lived in a big house on the club grounds but Mrs. Hurbaugh was getting sick and with the children grown and gone, they sold it. The kitchen was never used in the apartment, consequently it was never outfitted and he Hurbaugh's took their meals in one of the many restaurants at the club. Many of his friends greeted us when we arrived, including many Palm Beach friends, that I recognized from the winter season in Palm Beach.

Mr. Hurbaugh's son and his friend met us at the apartment and we all went to dinner at one of the many downstairs dining rooms. The next day, the son took me shopping at an upscale mall for kitchen equipment. His son also shopped at Tiffany's Jewelry, purchasing expensive gifts for the church secretary, etc., introducing me as, "Ms. Tiffany," and requesting that I show my identity credit cards. I was so embarrassed and quickly left the shop ahead of him. He said that I should buy anything that I wanted because, as he said, "He will be dead soon, so get what you want." I did not purchase anything from Tiffany's but we did purchase kitchen equipment from another store. I really needed to make the kitchen complete to allow Mr. Hurbaugh to entertain small dinner parties. Well, it soon became the "in place" to be invited for dinner parties.

The table sat just six people, including Mr. Hurbaugh and the parties were always on Mondays as this was when the club dining facilities were closed. One couple, in their late nineties, asked if he would entertain them on another night and he laughingly replied that he only entertained on the evening the club dining rooms were closed. Mr. Hurbaugh did so enjoy the summer season and his sudden notoriety as the perfect host. I trained a staff member at the club how to serve as butler, I cooked all the foods for the dinners, set the table and managed to do some wonderful things out of this small kitchen. I did so enjoy watching Mr. Hurbaugh come to life during this time. He had so many friends, some very well-known, and just the most amazing people. They, like we say in England, just "clicked."

Mr. Hurbaugh's daughter had a wonderful summer home on the Jersey shore and rented a house on the ocean for her father, myself and the rest of the family. To get Mr. Hurbaugh to the ocean in his car was quite a project due to his claustrophobia, but we made it. What a wonderful place, as I had no idea that New Jersey had such a fabulous coast line, with Stone Harbour right at the end of the parkway. We were to spend a few weeks there, and the rest of his family was to join us, including his son and his friend, and his other daughter with her friend, and young children. Everything was great but I was left to do all the work and it really got to me. I purchased the food across the other side of the bay (because this was an island), cooked, washed and served. I told Mr. Hurbaugh that certain members of the family were not pulling their weight as it had originally been arranged and he gave all of them a good piece of his mind, reminding them that I was not there to be chief cook and bottle washer. I was not exactly loved by the son or his daughter and her friend at the time and they did not take threats by Mr. Hurbaugh seriously.   I then appealed to his daughter who had a real screaming match with them and said that she would take care of them, one day.

The one daughter and son-in-law gave such fun filled parties for lifeguards as well as their friends. In fact, the daughter used to take lunch to the lifeguards every day. Their next door neighbors, Mr. and Mrs. Reese owned the well-known chocolate company that made Reese's Peanut Butter cups and later, when we returned to Florida, I made a cheesecake with their peanut butter cups as part of the ingredients. There was one party in which all on deck helped make the hors d'oeuvres and even the son-in-law's parents participated. There was much laughing and talking, but the son and his friend did not participate as I guess it was not quite their kind of fun. The father- in- law was the official bartender, in bare feet as this was a beach house, and I showed the son-in-law how to strip a filet of beef of its' silverskin and side strap to make a beautiful roast that he was able to grill.

I must tell you that one night we had cooked lobsters brought to the house and laid out newspapers instead of tablecloths. They came with lots of melted butter, potatoes and corn on the cob. I told everyone not to suck on the carcasses or legs as I wanted to use them the next day to make stock for lobster bisque. So, they put everything into a special bowl and next day I made lobster stock with plenty of cognac and vegetables to make beautiful lobster bisque for the evening meal. All I had to do was get two more lobsters for their meat since it had all been eaten the previous night.

It was a great summer for most of us, and we'd go out for dinner now and again, although some family members had other things planned. Mr. Hurbaugh, his daughter, son-in-law and his parents, the children, and I went to such wonderful restaurants in Cape May. The Jersey shore was such an awakening for me. Cape May is a beautiful Edwardian town with lots of gorgeous homes, restaurants, and hotels.

Now, we were back in New York where I was preparing for vacation in England with my son, John. John arrived at the airport and we returned to the club where Mr. Hurbaugh had arranged a room for him. The Buick Classic golf tournament was in progress at the club, so the place was busy. My son, John worked as club manager for a private club in Florida owned by Wayne Huizenga, owner of the Miami Dolphins. The guests at Mr. Huizenga's club were invited to play golf and join in all the other activities arranged by my son. These guests were often brought in by private helicopters and included presidents, royalty and heads of foreign countries. Well, my son was immediately recognized and embraced by several professional golf players who regularly played as guests at the club in Florida, asking John, "What the devil are you doing here?" or something similar to that, so my son explained about our trip to England and then introduced them to our host, Mr. Hurbaugh. I have photographs of Tiger Woods on the putting green, taken from right outside my bedroom window. Next day, John and I were taken to the airport for our departure to England, where both John and I had been born, as mentioned in previous chapters. We left as Mr. Hurbaugh would be taken care of by just about every club and staff member until my return. I had a wonderful time with my family and old friends in England. John and I also visited many places which held good memories for us both. Then, all too soon, it was back to the club for me to be met by Mr. Hurbaugh, who was very happy to see me and to return to our normal, fun filled routine.

I was a member of the Fancy Food Show, so as British House Ltd., I requested four tickets with our names as buyers so that I could take Mr. Hurbaugh, his daughter, son-in -law, and myself to the show at the Convention Center in New York City. Mr. Hurbaugh would follow a little later and Joe would drive him in the car since walking around the vast center with vendors from all over the world would tire him. The rest of us went on the train and arranged to meet him in the front lobby a few hours later. I think the son-in-law tried every mustard there was on the planet and religiously filled out a comment form. Meanwhile, Mr. Hurbaugh's daughter and I browsed. She saw some wicker picnic and wine baskets, commenting they would make great Christmas gifts and I explained to her, that as buyers she could purchase them at cost and have them shipped to her home. She listened as I talked to venders about business and in no time flat, she had the courage to do her own talking. Venders asked, "What does your company do?' and she replied," We do welcome baskets for very upmarket homes in Palm Beach." Now she had their attention, noting the Palm Beach million dollar homes as she placed a large order to be shipped under British House. Meanwhile in the lobby, there were autograph hunters looking for the latest food channel stars to sign their latest book.

I saw my friend, Carolyn O'Neal, who worked for Ted Turner at CNN, chatting with Bobby Flay, and she saw me and came over to give me a big hug. We had not seen each other for donkey's years so I quickly told her what had transpired with Dick. Carolyn said it was such a shame that Dick had hindered my career. Never mind, at least Bert Wolf did a good job as Ted Turner's food expert, instead of me, as I explained in the Bon Appétit Chapter. I introduced Carolyn to my crew with me and she in turn introduced us to many of the stars in the lobby by their names. That was a red letter day for the family meeting all those famous foodies. I took Mr. Hurbaugh, who had arrived with Joe, and left the others to contemplate their next purchases. Mr. Hurbaugh and I walked down the aisle of French booths so he could taste the cheeses, pates, caviars and wines. This was quite enough walking for him so we returned to the front where Joe was waiting to take him to the Pierre Hotel to relax over a cocktail and we were to join him later.

The show closed and there were no taxis, limos or buses available, so we were lined up waiting, until Mr. Hurbaugh's son-in-law said, "Follow me, I have an idea." He knew the city like the back of his hand. So, we followed him up a side street and were told to wait while he went across to the right hand side where horses and carriages were kept after they had finished their walks in Central Park. I have no idea what he did or how much it cost but suddenly a horse was hooked up to its carriage ready to drive us through the city to the Pierre Hotel in royal style. I said, "let's wave to everyone like the Queen does," and as this was not the normal route the horses took, people stared as they saw two silly women waving like maniacs. When we walked inside the Pierre, we saw a couple of tarts chatting up Mr. Hurbaugh, so we took another look, then took him by the arm saying, "'Come on, Dad, we are here for dinner," so the women quietly slipped away. We had a great dinner despite all the rich food we had tasted all day and happily slipped off our shoes in the car with our dogs barking (feet aching) back to the apartment.

Now, it was the end of the summer season and Joe packed the car with our hand baggage ready for the airport. The date was 9/11 and we had first class tickets from New York to West Palm Beach. Our personal luggage had already gone and I was watching TV while waiting for Joe when I saw what I thought was a small plane just touching the top of the Twin Towers, and said to myself, "How stupid these incompetent pilots are to hit this tall tower," not realizing how really serious it was. I turned off the TV as we then left for the airport. While Joe was driving, a call came from my son, Tommy, the fire chief in Florida, saying that we had better go back, there was something bad happening in New York, but Mr. Hurbaugh said, "Oh, we'll be ok, when we reach the airport's gold crown room, we'll hang out there," so I handed over my phone and listened. Mr. Hurbaugh then told Joe that we had to immediately return to the apartment as the bridges and roads were all closed and thank goodness we did or otherwise we would have been stranded somewhere in New York. Now, we were back at the apartment but my clothes were already in Florida, though Mr. Hurbaugh had a complete wardrobe at the club and another in Florida.

196

Within a week, it began to get cooler and I had no warm clothes so Mr. Hurbaugh suggested I buy some.

There were special services held at the club for twelve young members who had lost their lives, leaving behind young children and wives. I had terrible feelings of being back in the war, watching smoke out of my bedroom window. I had flashbacks to the war years, became emotional and found myself calling my family every day which I did not realize until my sons mentioned it to each other. We were able to leave for Florida three weeks later when the airport reopened and flights were available. While at the airport, it was quite eerie because hardly anyone was there. I had never seen the airport so quiet. I went around the stores and found some globes of scenes of New York with the Twin Towers. You shook the globe and snow would appear to be falling but it reminded me of all of the debris falling from the Towers. I bought some as mementos for my family and Mr. Hurbaugh's.

As we settled in on the plane, we were offered drinks and Mr. Hurbaugh chose vodka and I had a diet soda. When we ordered dinner, we were given regular forks but with plastic knives, which was not easy in cutting a steak. In regular class, passengers were offered great sandwiches that I wish we had had. There began the withholding of real dinner knives for plastic ones since you could stab someone with a real dinner knife, if that was your intention.

Settling back in the house on Jupiter Hills was no problem except when I realized Mr. Hurbaugh was no longer able to shower and dress. I came down one night to find him walking around telling me that Mrs. Hurbaugh was caught in the fireplace and we must help to get her out. I followed him, with his hands full of soot, into his den and saw that he had thrown rose petals over the electric fireplace and said that I must help get her out. The medications were obviously having an effect on his brain. He had an appointment every week with a physician

197

well knowledgeable with Parkinson's disease but it was not safe anymore to leave him downstairs alone, so I had to find somebody to help me with him. Finally after tryouts with many whose English was not good, we found a very nice gentleman named Everton, from Jamaica, who could help Mr. Hurbaugh shower and dress. What a joy, and caring.

We found a week-day male nurse named Sean and needed a male nurse for weekends. I had just about given up, when I found a wonderful nurse, Monica, for the weekends and she was great. She helped Mr. Hurbaugh but he would not let her bathe him or dress him. So, his male nurse would do this before going off duty. Now, we were ok, and most nights I was able to sleep well. I worried about Mr. Hurbaugh and in finding suitable nurses but now it seemed that after all these tryouts, we were set. Unfortunately, we were unable to spend summers at his New York home and I knew he missed his friends. We settled on the fact that this was his full time home now and his family would have to visit him here. My son, Tommy, dressed in his fire chief's uniform, would come to have lunch at the club at Mr. Hurbaugh's invitation when he was out checking one of the sixteen fire stations and emergency helicopters under his command.

Mr. Hurbaugh's daughter and son-in-law had been delaying a trip to England because of her father's health. They were planning to stay in England on business for a couple years. I told them, "Don't worry about him, I'll take care of him and never leave him alone, after all you are only a telephone call away." I had a very special lady named Doris who came in on my day off, and took good care of Mr. Hurbaugh, even driving him to any appointments.

I spoke to my sister in Yorkshire, and she arranged with the lady Member of Parliament who had taken our father's place in the House of Commons, to give them a royal tour of Parliament instead of having to go through the public entrance and a long line. I have the letters pertaining to this from the MP. She also very graciously arranged for the son-in-law to attend a private dinner at Buckingham Palace with Prince Charles. He was to be with other business men from all over the world. Of course, he called me next day to boast how he and Charlie were now good friends and he even met Camilla. Mr. Hurbaugh's daughter wished that she could have gone too, but it was for men only. So, the next best thing I thought would be for my sister Janice to arrange for her to go to Ascot. Janice got her into the royal enclosure at Ascot with a few of her friends. I said to her,"You must hire your hats for this occasion, don't buy them." She later called from England and said she could have touched the Queen.

One time when I was speaking to Mr. Hurbaugh's daughter in England, she laughingly told me that she had had a flat tire so a man changed it for her and said that she had better call a store for a replacement. So, she looked in the yellow pages but could not see the adverts for tires, because the word in England is spelled tyres. When they returned to the U.S., sooner than had been planned, there were tears on the plane which led the air hostess to enquire if everything was ok, and she was told that they were upset to have to leave England. We hoped life would get better with some adjustments and enjoyable for Mr. Hurbaugh, but it was not to be.

Previously, I had taken Mr. Hurbaugh to the hospital and as he had developed pneumonia, I called the family and the only member that could come down immediately was Mr. Hurbaugh's son. He came and decided to begin making arrangements to place his father as a permanent resident in a nursing home, where he could go for therapy and regain his strength after leaving the hospital. I immediately contacted a good friend and adviser of Mr. Hurbaugh's and explained the situation because Mr. Hurbaugh kept saying, "Take me home, take me home." So, I told this good friend, "Look we have all these nurses; we have everything needed for his

rehabilitation, with therapists, etc, so we should take him home."
I think Mr. Hurbaugh's son saw an opportunity to get his father
out of the way, and me, too, as I interfered with this son's plans.
Why, he even called his lover and told him that I had locked
him out of the house. I told the pastor that this was
impossible as his son was using Mr. Hurbaugh's convertible
which had the garage and house code in it. And, seeing how I
lived above the garage, I could hear the doors open and close.

Mr. Hurbaugh's nurse was with him at the nursing home,
so it was only the son and me at the house, or so I thought. The
son began bringing young men into the house. Cheryl, the
housekeeper, told me, "Someone's been in the nursery," and she
could tell even though I couldn't. Then, Mr. Hurbaugh was
able to come home and Everton saw young men leaving the
kitchen and going up the front stairs; he investigated and found
several young men wandering around the house. I called Mr.
Hurbaugh's daughter and let her know of the situation and she
soon got her brother out of there. You know, I am extremely
broad minded but what the son was doing to his father and to his
own lover was despicable, never mind his atrocious lies about
me.

Out of the blue, Mr. Hurbaugh's son called and said that
he was coming down, so he could spend some time with his
father, maybe hit a few golf balls together. When the son
arrived, he made himself at home, moved furniture around,
changed light bulbs to a lower wattage and with pink tint,
until I stopped him from touching the downstairs, including
Mr. Hurbaugh's suite. After all, Mr. Hurbaugh needed all the
light he could get, especially so with macular degeneration.
When the son arrived, he said to Mr. Hurbaugh that he was
sending his father's driver with a limousine to pick up a golf
professional at the airport. I told Mr. Hurbaugh, "Let him go
pick up this person himself, instead of trying to impress him by
sending a chauffeur in a limousine." I went to my apartment
after dinner leaving Mr. Hurbaugh with his nurse and the son

had already left for the airport in the convertible. The next morning, when I was in the kitchen cooking Mr. Hurbaugh's breakfast, his son walked in and set up a breakfast tray for two, very formal and included flowers. The night before I had made fresh fruit salad, so he put two full dishes on the tray looking very festive, made coffee and took the tray upstairs for his guest and himself. Meanwhile, I went shopping for stone crabs, in season then, and other groceries. When I returned to the house, Cheryl came out to talk to me.

The son's golf pro apparently arrived with no golf clubs, shoes or regular golfing gear or the normal style clothes needed for visiting the club dining room. The guys had visited the Ritz Carlton Spa as Mr. Hurbaugh had a membership then, so they jolly well made sure use of it. I went to see Mr. Hurbaugh in his library and said, "I thought you would be out hitting a few balls," whereupon he told me the guys had left him and there he was sitting in his golf shoes. I was furious, which only increased when I went upstairs with the housekeeper and found every bedroom had been used. Towels were everywhere along with empty Dom Perignon champagne bottles. Cheryl took me into the bedroom the couple had used and pointed out some things on the dressing table and then, I nearly died laughing. Cheryl showed me the guest's clothing, he had no type of clothes to use for the club and as of yet, I had not seen this guy. Finally, Mr. Hurbaugh's son and a much younger man arrived carrying a full set of new golf clubs, expensive shirts, shorts and pants, all bought at Mr. Hurbaugh's club house. I checked with the golf shop and found out that Mr. Hurbaugh's account balance was now quite a few thousand dollars more. Of course, right away I realized what was going on. The guest had a first class ticket back to where the son and the reverend apparently lived but not on the same flight that the son was booked on. Apparently, he sent young teenage boys from his church postcards with buxom women on them saying, "'See what you are missing in Florida" and these were open postcards for anyone to see including the parents of these young boys.

All the time that I was employed at this house, I did not let the son's partner know what was going on. Believe me, this took some doing because whenever the couple came together for family gatherings with the children and the grandchildren, it became harder and harder. His son tried very hard to get me to leave but Mr. Hurbaugh's oldest daughter and husband, the ones that lived in England, knew all the details of what was happening and there was no way they would let me go, because I promised to stay with their father as long as he lived. My employer was now being fed via stomach tube, no more solid food and he did love to eat. I used to grind his medication very fine to mix with his special adult liquid food. I was not a nurse but one came by every week to check on him and I soon learned how to feed him. Mr. Hurbaugh never wanted me to see him in a state of undress but he had a bad case of diarrhea so I had to help Everton get him into the shower in the wheelchair and Everton had to shower, too. I was outside the shower ready with warm towels for both of them. Mr. Hurbaugh would have been upset for me to see him in this state.

The nurse came to check on Mr. Hurbaugh and said his pneumonia had returned and suggested we go to the hospital. Mr. Hurbaugh looked at her and said, "No," then looked at me and said, "You will take care of me won't you?" And I said, "Of course!" The nurse made a note of the conversation and nodded her head. It was a weekend and no doctors could be easily found to authorize oxygen, so my son arranged for oxygen since taking him to the hospital was out of the question. Hospice was to come and visit him the next week and time was now short for him so I called the family to come to Florida. The children and grandchildren came but I told them not to eat in the house because the smell of the food might upset Mr. Hurbaugh.

Mr. Hurbaugh slept most of the time now as his body was slowly shutting down. He was sleeping when the family came in again before leaving for home so there were no final goodbyes.

When he awoke, I told him that he was sleeping so soundly that none of them wished to waken him, and I asked if he would like to talk to them and he said, "Of course!" So, I called the daughter and her husband a few minutes later, Mr. Hurbaugh talked to them and then wanted to talk to his granddaughter, telling her how he wanted to dance at her wedding and then said that he felt so tired so they must make plans tomorrow. I placed the phone back on the receiver and helped make him more comfortable. Mr. Hurbaugh settled on his back and I told him that I would put the baseball game on for him to watch with Sean.

I went into the kitchen with Cheryl and just a few moments later, Sean came in and said that Mr. Hurbaugh had just died. Cheryl and I rushed into his bedroom, checked his pulse and realized that he was gone. I telephoned the family, as some had not yet returned home, I got his daughter and son- in-law on the phone and told them. I called my son, Tommy, and he came over right away, telling me not to touch a thing as he was sending paramedics over to take Mr. Hurbaugh's vital signs. I placed at the base of the bed an order from the family not to resuscitate, as this was not the way that he wished to live.

There were no narcotics in the house but the police department came and took all of Mr. Hurbaugh's medications. When Tommy arrived, he called the funeral home. I knew the owners of the funeral home and they had met the Hurbaugh family earlier. The following day was the viewing and all three of my sons were ushers. Tommy was in his full dress uniform which he did not often wear as it had much brass and ribbons, but he did so in memory of Mr. Hurbaugh. Then, two days later was the funeral and once more my sons were ushers. Mr. Hurbaugh's son had a great voice and sang the Lord's Prayer. I, along with others, felt he had no remorse and honestly felt he was a devil and his god was money. We did not go to the cemetery as just the family went there. But all were invited back to the club for a wonderful lunch in his honor. Family, friends and other people who had worked for him came to pay respect.

Right after Mr. Hurbaugh passed away, his son- in- law arrived with his family and as he was one of the executors of the will, he asked me what I would like and I told him that I would love to have the bedroom set from one of the guests rooms and when he asked me which car that I would like, I told him the Lincoln, and he said, "Consider it done!" Well, when the son arrived with his lover, the minister, he had a hissy fit over it but what could he do? It was already promised. So he decided to make life hell for me as much as he could.

I went out to purchase some food, as the whole family was eating at the house while packing the family treasures. The little ones wanted certain foods that I had prepared for them through the years, such as Shepherd's pie (recipe included) and Clayton loved my English chocolate cookies which soon would become a memory but at least Mr. Hurbaugh's daughter had the Shepherd's pie recipe and will use it for years to come. I arrived back at the house with groceries to start baking and cooking. Well, there was a large dumpster outside to put out what they did not want to keep, and the son took all the foods that I had made out of the freezer, dishes included, and threw the whole mess into the dumpster. So childlike, as they would be in residence until the house was cleared out, and that would have enabled them to enjoy good food without having to go out and eat.

My son, Tommy, suggested to the family that if they donated the golf cart to the county fire department, it would be a good tax write off. They had helicopters for medical emergencies and to supply the helicopters they had to have a vehicle to take medical supplies to the helicopter. The family was happy to see the cart would be put to such good use and my son had an emblem placed on the golf cart with Mr. Hurbaugh's name on it as a dedication. By the way, a double whammy happened during the hurricane season as never in the history of the hurricane season did two storms hit the same area within weeks of one another. They managed to get all of the helicopters out to a safe area but the golf cart was left behind. After these hurricanes were gone, the helicopter hanger was a mess but the golf cart survived. It didn't even have a scratch on it. So we figured Mr. Hurbaugh was up there looking down on us and that it was a miracle. I have pictures of the helicopter and the golf cart. Mr. Hurbaugh's son and his lover left New Jersey and now reside in California. If only the good people in their new church knew what they were up to when they were in Florida. But never mind, that is another story and I am sure my mother would have said that they will get their comeuppance (their dues) one of these days.

SHEPHERD'S PIE

3 tbsp. oil
2 medium chopped onions
1 ½ lbs. ground beef or lamb
2 tbsp. flour
1 ½ cups beef stock
2 tbsp. steak sauce
Salt & pepper

Mash potatoes; not too creamy. Use butter. Pinch nutmeg, salt and pepper.
In heavy bottom saucepan, add oil, then chopped onion (slightly brown). Remove and add meat to brown, mix well all the time. Add flour, now gradually add stock and steak sauce, stir, medium heat. Cook meat mixture approximately 1 hour. Strain mix. Keep a little sauce in it. Keep gravy to serve separately. Place in an ovenproof baking dish and top with potatoes. Seal edges. Use a fork to decorate top. Place on butter blogs. Place in hot oven or microwave to heat. Place under broiler to brown top.

DEEP FRIED MARS BARS

(Use Snickers if Mars Bars unavailable)

Egg Roll skins
Chocolate syrup
Deep Fryer
Fresh Oil
Powdered sugar.

Cut bars into 3. Place each on eggroll skin diagonal. Fold one point over the bar. Wet edges and fold over other edge, and then fold over seal like making egg rolls. Freeze 1 hour.
Deep fry 350 degrees, turn over to cook just till brown. Drain and place on plate. Drizzle syrup on top, then sieve the sugar on top of plate. Serve hot.

Chapter
19 THE OLD SALT

The elderly Mr. Berndt looked the part of either a pirate or an old sailor who had been at sea too long. He never wore shoes except for old deck shoes when he went out. He was everything one could imagine a sailor was and would do; he never shaved and was unlike any client that I had ever worked for. How did I get this job? My agent called and told me about Mr. Berndt and I must admit I was intrigued as I had never worked for such an unusual person, quite an exception to the normal "Palm Beach" client. I thought about it, and then went for the interview anyway. I actually thought it might be fun being from the other side of the track and I think my agent was offering me a change of pace; no pretentiousness.

I was very curious and when I saw Mr. Berndt's house in Jupiter Hills, it was so unusual and not a bit like any other estate that I had seen. Just the waterfront and the gazebo would be hard to explain to the average person, as it was hard enough for me to get myself wrapped around this place. It was on the water, not on the ocean, and quite an estate that I would say was not considered normal in any decorator's book.

Inside the house was a hodgepodge collection of furniture, suits of medieval armor, pirate chests, real elephant's feet used as cocktail tables, rhinoceros feet, animal hides on the floor, including a lion's hide. Mr. Berndt smoked Cuban cigars both inside the house as well as outside in the gazebo. The gazebo was refurnished by Seminole Indians during the time that I was employed there and probably without obtaining permits. Mr. Berndt had two beautiful dogs; one was a poodle, which had his left eye accidentally shot out while Mr. Berndt was squirrel hunting at his Carolina house. The house held quite a collection of guns, both antique and new.

In Mr. Berndt's living room was a cannon from the Nuestra Senora Atocha, a ship that sank in an atrocious storm on September 6, 1662. What was this cannon doing there, you might ask? Well, here it was after lying at the bottom of the sea, found around tons of gold and silver being carried by the Atocha. I was told that Mel Fisher was a friend of Mr. Berndt, and had asked his old buddy to help finance the ship's excavation and was reimbursed (after the government received their share) with gold bars, silver and many artifacts. Coins from the days of Kings Philip II and III were discovered and shoveled onto the salvage ship. Mr. Berndt gave me three silver coins, one for each of my boys, with a signed document proving the coins' authenticity, as many have been forged for tourist shops. Many of these artifacts were brought to the surface on July 20, 1985. Mr. Berndt had been involved in many successful financial business ventures, including real estate.

I accepted the job with the understanding from him that I wear blue jeans and T-shirts; no formal wear and his food requests were normal, nothing fancy or pretentious. After being there a few weeks, Mr. Berndt asked to talk with me and he said, "Pauline, girl, you are a damn good cook." End of conversation. I had an apartment in what had been a game room in the basement but was now outfitted with a bathroom and Murphy bed.

There was one small but important fact that my agent neglected to divulge to me and that was the fact that Mr. Berndt had been divorced, then remarried to a much younger woman of which his daughter and husband did not approve of as whatever fortune they were to inherit after their father's death would now be shared with the young bride. This, of course, was a major cause of tension. The son-in-law apparently wanted his father-in-law to give him one of his boats but the new wife said, "No," so he left for his own home just down the street. Meanwhile, Mrs. Berndt was up on a ladder decorating the top tier of their

Christmas tree when the son-in-law stormed in with his gun, pointed it at her and shot her dead.

After the son-in-law was sent to jail for the murder of his mother-in-law, his wife, Laurie, allowed *his* son, by previous marriage I presume, to move in with her and take over as man of the house. Mr. Berndt was not aware of this and thought that the young man was just visiting. He was not a boy but much younger than Laurie and since Mr. Berndt never visited the house that he had bought for Laurie when she married, the two men never crossed paths. When they cleaned up the house after the murder, they left behind a bullet embedded in the wall going up the stairs to the dining room, so I placed a statue in front of it to cover it up.

The hurricane season was about to hit and boy oh boy, it hit with a vengeance. Mr. Berndt had a generator and after being given advance warning from my son, the Martin County Fire and Emergency Services Chief, I was able to cook and stock the freezers and refrigerators with enough food to feed an army. Mr. Berndt invited many friends to join him and keep him company while I, at the insistence of my son, went home to my family.

My poor Jaguar (my pride and joy) was battered by the high gale force winds but I managed to avoid tree branches, weaving in and out of the way. There was no traffic, thank goodness, as the first of the rain gusts was arriving. I arrived home to a house full of family members. John already had the generator charged up and ready when the power failed. After the storm came, snakes slithered out of their nests uprooted from under the trees so we had to wear boots if we went outside. One lady neighbor came out in her yard in bare feet and guess what? She was bit by a rattlesnake. The ambulance was called and managed to get through a tangled mess of road to take care of her. There were other victims, too, including a man bit by a wild pig. All the wild creatures were in a tizzy and upset as much as the humans. Our dog and cat stayed pretty calm, curled up on a bed with one of us for company. The electricity was out and the generator not quite big enough to handle all we needed, so like everyone else, we fired up the grill outside to cook as much food as possible before it spoiled. With the strong gale winds there was no sleeping for anyone.

The eye of the storm came over us and it was so strange and quiet, no birds were singing as the animals knew only too well there was more to come. We went outside to do some damage repair and cut down a few tree limbs about ready to fall on the roof. The storm started up again with wind gusts reversing but it eventually stopped and we again surveyed the damage. Actually, our house survived pretty well but many of our neighbors were without a roof and water damage ruining their possessions. Garage doors were ripped off and homes were unlivable. My son, Paul's house was located in the first area to get electricity back on since it was on the hospital, jail and emergency services line, so we took showers after four days without running water at his house. We had plenty of drinking water and the bathtubs were loaded with water ready for flushing toilets and quick washes to at least make us easy to live with, and we had talcum powder and perfumes.

I then headed back to a house full of guests at Mr. Berndt's and quickly helped get the place back in order but why worry? The most unusual thing happened as another hurricane came bearing down on us just a few weeks later. This had never happened before with two hurricanes heading for the same place. Well, my son, the chief, certainly had his hands full and once more we did what we did during the last hurricane. Finally, I again returned to my apartment at Mr. Berndt's but the ceiling tiles were soaking wet and by then, I felt sick and could not breathe. When I told Mr. Berndt, he was unsympathetic, but I knew there was something wrong so I went to his daughter, Laura, and told her I had to leave and to advise her father of the situation and she did. I left and called my doctor, Dr. Kardos, who then sent me to get a chest x-ray. I had been to Palm Beach and was on my way back home when my cell phone rang and it was the doctor. She asked me where I was and when I told her I was on Interstate 95, she asked me to come see her. When I arrived at her office, Dr. Kardos told me that cancer was present in both lungs, and two more tests confirmed that the right front lobe and part of the left front lobe should be removed.

It takes quite a lot to defeat me and I forged ahead with Dr. Sunil Gandhi, my lung physician, taking great care of me. If there is one good thing that comes out of telling you about my cancer is that if you have a great surgeon and a fabulous back-up physician, then this disease can be treated but time is of the essence, especially if you smoke. I quit smoking just before working at C'est Si Bon, feeling the influence from Dick slowly leaving me. It is marvelous what a change in your life can do. I used cigarette smoking as a crutch to get me through all my ups and downs of that stage in my life and now must pay yet another heavy price with my health.

No, friends, this was not in any way the end of my career, as my career continued after a long, boring recuperation since I am not the kind of person who thrives on bad health and sympathy. I was soon ready to get back to work and anyone just looking at me would never know that I had health problems. However, I did decide not to work full time but my love of cooking was still as strong as ever, especially so in my next job.

Chapter

20 THE PESLARS

The expression, 'Build it and they will come' from the movie *Field of Dreams* does not pertain to estates built by top architects for new people trying to get into Palm Beach society. I was asked by my agent to go for an interview at a new estate on the ocean and the couple to meet and interview me was the estate manager and his wife who lived in a small cottage next to the main house. This cottage was by any standards top class costing a million or two, but was in keeping with new estate's staff quarters.

I pulled into the drive next to three garages and met the estate manager, Wayne, and his wife, Fran. She was very petite and he towered over her. Wayne had worked for the FBI and been a bodyguard for Richard Nixon. Now retired, he was manager, butler and jack of all trades to the Peslars. Fran, his wife, was in charge of the housekeeper and laundress and also helped the family. They were looking for a chef just for the weekends, since they travelled back and forth between two homes. Mr. Peslar was a car parts manufacturer for big automobile plants and the family came down only on the weekends at this time. The estate manager had no problem with my resume and proceeded to take me on the grand tour which by the way, would be my only time above stairs as I was their chef and had no other business upstairs.

We walked up winding stone stairs to see bedrooms and dressing rooms. The whole house had been professionally decorated with very few homey, personal touches. It was the classic cookie cutter Palm Beach style that I had seen many years in Palm Beach. Madam's walk in clothes closet and massive dressing room was full of top designer clothes in a couple of different sizes, so if Madam was to put on a few more pounds it would not be obvious, though, please understand that I had not met the family as yet and the only photographs seen on the cocktail and end tables were of their daughter, Bethany, riding her horses, but none of the family. Since it was only a weekend position, my job did not include living quarters, so I stayed with my girlfriend, Karol, to cut down on driving time and spend more time with my old friend.

Just down the road was Mar -a –Lago, owned by Donald Trump, and two other estates mentioned in past chapters, that of Rod Stewart and Sidney Kimmel. The Peslar house was featured in Architectural Digest and on its front cover was a photograph of the master bedroom. It has only been recently that homes on South Ocean Boulevard have had their interiors photographed for fear of being burglarized and households are now more apt to use security systems as before, burglaries occurred more often when staff or residents neglected to use these aids.

By the way, my employment agent was also responsible for placing Wayne and Fran, with the Peslar's. And, the Peslar's house keeper now works for Fred Couples, the famous golfer. I also worked for a famous golfer but just for a few weeks. His name was Raymond Floyd and I was supposed to replace the chef except that they also wanted me as housekeeper, which was not to my liking.

I was given a list of the Peslar's food requests for the following weekend which included hash browns for the daughter, to be made like McDonalds (a first for me), pasta sauce to be picked up by Wayne from a small Italian restaurant in West Palm Beach, French pastries commercially made from a local pastry shop (I know the real thing), pancakes (dollar size and they did mean dollar size as I carefully measured them to make sure they made the grade), then the rest was left up to me

213

for their first dinner. No wonder Wayne and Fran were a little uptight as they relayed messages to me.

Bethany and her female companion were to be joining the Peslar's on every visit as the girl was into horses and her father had bought her a fully equipped stable in Wellington next to the grounds where Prince Charles used to play polo. This stable area had its own paddocks, trainers and stable hands. I swear that it was grander than many estates. Wayne would take the two girls out there and return later to pick them up, stopping at McDonalds on the way back so they could nosh (eat) on fries and burgers, getting rid of the evidence before the car was returned to the garages and there Fran would quickly spray the inside with deodorizer.

I started the following weekend arriving early only to be met by Fran telling me to remove my shoes and quietly creep into the kitchen without uttering a sound as Madam would have a fit if she was awakened. I crept in with groceries clinging to my body and praying that I would not drop them, thinking no wonder this was an uptight household. Well, it was weekends only for me and the pay was excellent, so since it was seasonal, I felt sure that I could handle the situation. I started very quietly preparing breakfast, but only got so far until the family put in an appearance. Mr. Peslar came downstairs to the kitchen and introduced himself. Fran had told me how nice he was and she was right. I gave him coffee as he waited and read the Shiny Sheet newspaper for all the latest Palm Beach gossip. No world news or important stock market reports in this paper, just photographs of people taken at the latest ball and everyone wanted to be in the Shiny Sheet.

Next to me, Fran began shaking in her boots as we heard the elevator descending. The doors were flung open and out came Madam, rather large, not the usual size six, and after all it is character that counts. Even Palm Beach had a few grand dames who were the life of the party and I knew quite a few of

214

these charming ladies. Fran quickly introduced me and then Mrs. Peslar went into the breakfast room for breakfast. Fran, bless her little cotton socks, told Mrs. Peslar about my resume and book with articles and photographs of my accomplishments, so Mrs. Peslar requested to see it. Now the damage was done because she saw what I could make. She summoned me into the breakfast room with requests for some of my desserts and entrees featured in the book. I could have strangled Fran but realized that this was a feather in her cap for finding me.

Mrs. Peslar inquired about the meaning behind the coronation salad and when I explained how it was named for Queen Elizabeth's coronation. The coronation service at Westminster Abbey was so long that chefs from the palace made this salad so the Queen, and her ladies in waiting, could slip back stage (so to speak) to take a nibble or two to keep up their stamina. Of course, Mrs. Peslar wanted this salad for lunch (recipe included). I made sticky buns regularly but without nuts in half as the daughter did not like nuts. Now came pastries like Petit Chocolate Eclairs, Mocha Profiteroles, Meringues Chantilly and lots of other food that she had seen photographs of in my book. No more store bought pastries, and the favorite of all was my Gateau au Chocolat (a Genoise split into six, each layer soaked in rum with a chocolate, butter cream filling) which was so rich. Then, for a change, the Gateau Mocha by the same process but filled with coffee butter cream filling.

All these weekends and I never saw any visitors and it was mid-season. It turns out the family was apparently not too popular even though they were members of the exclusive Everglades Club where only WASP's were allowed. According to Wayne, they only went there a couple of times. The last time, upon leaving the club, Mrs. Peslar was in tears at their being shunned by the members and they never went back. As I said, just because you build a new home in Palm Beach does not mean that you are accepted.

The kitchen windows overlooked the pool and the ocean. I was so used to being at the ocean, having owned and lived at the Alexandra Hotel in England; we had three acres of private lawn leading down to the ocean.

One morning, as I tiptoed into the kitchen, I went to open the wood shutters and realized they would not open. Wayne quietly appeared so I asked him why the shutters would not open and he replied that Mrs. Peslar did not want any of us to see her in the pool or in the ocean. Wow. You could have blown me over with a feather.

When Madam came down in the elevator, this elevator warned us of her appearance as the noise it made was our cue that Madam was about to grace us with her presence. Everyone patiently waited for her complaints to Wayne and Fran about the housekeeping or the outside windows that were forever covered with spray from the ocean which she ordered Wayne to take care of it right away.

On this particular morning she made a detour to the kitchen to tell me that they were invited out for dinner at the Judge's house and she needed a Mocha Gateau. I really had to get busy then as this took quite a few hours to bake and put together so I turned on the mixer to beat up the eggs and sugar. Suddenly, Madam came storming into the kitchen with eyes glowering at me and asked what I was doing making all this noise while she was having breakfast. There seemed not much use in trying to explain to her that if she was to get her Gateau, then I had to begin preparing it now. So, I asked Wayne to help me pick up my pastry station and follow me outside to the barbeque grill area where there was electricity and a small table attached to the grill. This was now the pastry department for today.

The Gateau was a great success but Mrs. Peslar was not the one to congratulate me. Wayne had driven them to the

Judge's house and heard Madam telling her husband that this was a red letter day for the family and by the way, the judge in question was not a regular judge but a horse show judge and they wanted to befriend him on behalf of their daughter. She was not good enough to make the big time even with Daddy's millions, but she was able to showcase her ribbons on the table in the front vestibule for all to see, though no one came to visit.

New Year's Eve happened to fall on a weekend and there would be fourteen guests so we got busy planning for this first great party. I worked with Madam on planning the menu and it was decided that Beluga 000 Caviar would be served with Petit Blinis to be passed along with Giant Shrimp and Cocktail Sauce plus Brie Hot Canapés which was my own concoction and the only thing the daughter would eat. Then the guests would sit down for a formal dinner of Cream of Mushroom Soup with fresh made Melba Toast, a salad of baby lettuces with my own Bon Appétit salad dressing. No fish or sorbet but right on to the Entrée of Grilled Filet of Beef (from the grill watched by Wayne and yours truly) served with a Béarnaise Sauce, Potato Roses and Petite Poise Sauce. Dessert was a huge Mocha Gateau, and I had to buy a larger than usual pan for this dessert.

The table was set and I helped make sure that all was in order for Wayne and Fran so we knew what we were doing. We were nervous about this affair, so ridiculous as here I (and they) were used to being in the company of VIP's and in serving royalty and presidents but somehow these people managed to keep us so uptight. There were no place cards for the table either, which was most unusual, I thought at the time. Mr. Peslar came downstairs in his tuxedo followed by Bethany and Laura in dresses obviously chosen by Madam as they were very young looking and too frilly for the both of them. Soon, the elevator descended and upon reaching the ground floor, the doors opened with Madam trying her best to get out.

She was truly stuck so Fran came to her rescue as Wayne and I disappeared out of the way (laughing our heads off). Madam's gown was a crinoline, encrusted with so much beading that she looked like Walt Disney World's Cinderella and she was also wearing a tiara. The only time tiaras were seen in Palm Beach was at the Red Cross Ball so this was a first for me. With a straight face, I came out (after her rescue from the elevator) and commentated on how regal she looked with all of her diamonds. She just smiled, not saying a word.

The guests arrived and what a surprise as they were all grooms and stable hands from Peslar's stables, in rented tuxedos with nervous wives appearing completely out of their element. I quickly told Wayne and Fran that these poor mites were like ducks out of water and to help them in any way they could on etiquette and service without Mr. and Mrs. Peslar's notice. Thank goodness we got through it all and they left the table after coffee. They waited for midnight by taking in the sights of a millionaire's mansion, perhaps the likes of which they had never seen before and probably wishing the night would end but could not escape until after midnight.

At last midnight struck with Wayne and Fran popping open champagne corks and passing champagne to the guests to toast in the New Year. Shortly after, guests began leaving with a thank you and a good night to the family. This was also my cue to leave and get home before any drunken revelers from other parties would be on the highway.

The Peslar's decided to leave Palm Beach earlier than originally planned. Mr. Peslar told me how much they had enjoyed my food and gave me a great reference. Sadly, he would die soon of cancer and the estate was sold.

CORONATION SALAD

Hold 3 lbs. cooked chicken breast in bite-sized pieces.

In a saucepan, add:
1 Medium onion – finely chopped
1 tbsp. olive oil
1 tbsp. curry powder. Cook one minute, then add:
½ cup chicken stock
2 tsp. tomato puree
2 tbsp. fresh lemon juice
3 tbsp. Mango Chutney. Cook approximately 10 minutes, then puree in the blender.
Cool and add: ½ cup mayonnaise
½ cup heavy cream

Place chicken pieces on a deep dish or bowl. Spoon over dressing. Serve with cold rice and a salad, with chopped parsley on top

BETHANY'S BRIE *HOR'S D'OEURVES*

Use store-bought frozen Phyllo Cups. Place a piece of room-temperature Brie in the cup. Press down. Top with light brown sugar. Heat. Can be done ahead of time and placed in freezer uncooked in the store-bought Phyllo cup holder. Then heat as needed. Add for a change on top - pepper jelly, spring onion, garlic jelly or other spicy toppings. Freeze and bring out to bake just until hot. For that quick cocktail party *H*or's D'oeurve.

Chapter

21 THE KIMMEL ESTATE

After my last season with Mr. and Mrs. Gilmour, I was offered a chance to interview for an estate manager, or "Major Domo" position with a large Canadian residential management services business where I was to reside and work on an estate in Palm Beach. I had my fill of travel experience in business to last my lifetime and did not wish to travel away from the area where my children and grandchildren lived. I had my fill with the rock and roll world, though I would not have missed the experience for the world.

Charles, the owner of the Canadian residential management services business, flew into Palm Beach to interview me at my agent's office. Charles and I were from the same school of training and we seemed to hit it off immediately. It was then arranged that I should meet with Sidney Kimmel in his office in New York. Apparently he had asked specifically for a female house manager and how refreshing it was for me to hear this after all these years fighting for my right as a female in a man's domain.

Mr. Kimmel's new estate had five acres of fabulous landscaping with a 32,000 square foot house on 300 feet of ocean and now all that it needed was the interior finishing. China was purchased from the Duke and Duchess of Windsor's estate via Sotheby's with all other first addition china collections from Dior, etc. There were sterling silver service and top of the line linens for bedrooms and different dining areas. There was a breakfast room with its own kitchen, there were outside private cottages which had to be furnished with kitchen appliances and china, etc. so that they were self contained and did not infringe on the main house. There was even a caterer's kitchen with a ramp to bring in food and a kitchen that was to die for! But, enough! As I am running away with myself!

Charles met me in New York at the airport before my meeting with Mr. Kimmel. I happened to own a Jones business suit and since Mr. Kimmel owned the company which made Jones attire, as well as several other retail clothing businesses, I thought it good luck to wear it. Charles briefed me in what to expect and said that this was one fine gentleman. Mr. Kimmel and Rena Rowan had lived together for twenty years, they co-founded Jones New York, but they never married. She is now married to singer Vic Damone but Mr. Kimmel was single at the time that I met him.

Charles repeated that Mr. Kimmel had requested a lady to handle his estate and I was ready to be interviewed. Charles would be sitting in on the meeting and the secretary took us into Mr. Kimmel's office. Mr. Kimmel was dressed casually, with shorts and a shirt as he said he had been working out in his gym attached to the office. I sat at the desk while Charles sat quietly behind me.

My resume and letters of recommendation were laid out in front of Mr. Kimmel as he began to question me and told me that he wanted a female estate manager that would take control. He asked, "Pauline, what would you think if a lady stayed over at my house as my guest, what would be your reaction?" and I said, "It is none of my business and I would treat the lady as I would any of your guests regardless of gender." He seemed to like my answer and we chatted some more. Finally, he came around his desk, shook my hand and said that he would be happy to have me take care of his estate, if that was ok with me? I said that was fine so he informed Charles to draw up the papers pertaining to my job, wages, etc. and I still have the agreement.

There were two fully furnished staff apartments and I was to occupy one of them. I went with my son, John, to purchase a car with a decent trunk that would hold enough luggage if sent to the airport for Mr. Kimmel's luggage so the limo would not be crowded and I would also need it for shopping and to be my house car. I did not live in at that time, as the house did not have its occupational license yet. So, I travelled from Stuart every day in my house car which had been paid in full by check. Charles stayed at the Four Seasons in Palm Beach while travelling back and forth between other jobs in Paris and London. His company was well known and he was in great demand.

Now, we had to begin hiring staff. I interviewed Nancy, a lady who loved to launder fine linens and a great seamstress, and she agreed to work with me (I never said worked for me) because it sometimes takes more than one to accomplish a task. Nancy was used to helping out with whatever was required.

Gary hired a professional computer wizard to take care of an extensive twenty-seven zone air conditioning system. The fact that Gary was Gregg Norman's brother-in-law with the best credentials did not hurt. At the front of the house was a button that one could press that would open up the bowels of the earth and swallow up the front and back glass panels. Not exactly true but the living room had twenty-six foot high ceilings and instead of walls there were twenty foot high glass panels that would disappear at the touch of a button into the floor, leaving the whole living room open to the elements of the ocean and pool.

The idea sounds great but consider this problem, what happens to fine paintings, including Picassos, the grand piano and other furniture and great artwork being exposed to salt air? I hoped the button would not be used too often as I cringed thinking wonders of the art could be ruined in this fashion.

There was a waterfall inside which covered a complete wall with water falling over handpicked pink rocks, all the same size, each one costing over $150 and there were more than a

222

thousand rocks.   In the front garden, there was another type of waterfall cascading downhill into a manmade pond winding over rocks and returning its journey back to the top of the garden. Someone had placed prime Kois into this pond with no word as how to take care of them and more importantly, no food.

Luckily, I had raised Kois at my restaurant, Bon Appétit. Back then, my ex-husband had purchased them and left me in charge to make sure the pond was clean, the waterfall scrubbed and the fish were fed.   The customer's children loved to feed them and were well distracted from misbehaving while dining at my four star restaurant, and cranky babies seemed to be soothed by the sound of the waterfall, falling asleep in portable cribs placed between chairs on the patio under the watchful eyes of staff and parents.

I worked my fanny off getting everything in place, as we heard that Mr. Kimmel was flying in on his private jet with the architect, Thierry Despont, who had also been the architect for Bill Gates. Charles was by my side awaiting their arrival when the front door opened and in stormed the architect while Mr. Kimmel was apparently detained out front talking with the landscape architect.

Thierry Despont glared at both Charles and I and then said, "Get the F--- out of here now both of you, I wish to talk to Sidney alone and don't need you SOB's here, and furthermore, I shall be here as a guest to get the kinks out of the property for quite a while, so the less I see of you two the better." Never in all of my life had I been talked to this way and I was flabbergasted at his crude language. Charles and I went upstairs to the staff apartments with poor Nancy saying to me that she quit and left out of the door. Sometime later, Despont called for Charles to come see him and off he went.

Charles later returned to the apartment and said to me, "Pauline, I have to let you go," and I asked, "Why?" and all

Charles could say was, "I'm sorry, it's politics." It took awhile to figure this all out as I was gob-smacked (speechless). I realized that even the owner who had flown me to New York for an interview had no control nor did he even realize that I was terminated since I would just disappear, leaving no telltale evidence that I had even worked there. I do remember that someone drove me home, as I had the house car and it needed to return to the estate. I was glad not to drive as I was shaking and therefore driving on busy Interstate 95 would have been an accident just waiting to happen.

I was not the only one fired as Charles got his walking papers, too, apparently, somehow not pleasing Mr. Kimmel's architect as well. After all the hard work that Charles had performed, he left leaving a job where he was owed many thousands of dollars and not reimbursed. Charles gave me a glowing reference, as he may have felt responsible for my first-ever sacking. If I had been younger, I would have enjoyed working with such a competent person such as Charles, anywhere in the world.

I remember when working with Eugene Lawrence, the architect at The Sun and Surf, who had also worked on Mar-a-Lago for Donald Trump, that nobody had ever heard cursing or shouting at any of the staff. This Thierry Despont person must have let his status go to his head and gave himself permission to do as he pleased.

Now, all I wanted to do was get this disappointment behind me and find another job in Palm Beach; with all my references and credentials, it would not be a problem.

In April 2008, Mr. Kimmel sold his estate for $85.1 million. He had finally married and moved to a smaller estate in Palm Beach.

In another chapter, you will see what happened when I met Mr. Kimmel again and with his new wife at the Toll residence in Palm Beach.

NO RECIPES AS NO COOKING

Chapter

22 THE TOLLS ESTATE

My agent, Gary, found me a part time position three days a week and after going through so much lung surgery in the recent past, I felt that three days was quite fine with me. My task was to prepare a few lunches and dinners, very simple and plain. The kitchen at this home was in the midst of renovation, had never been used and none of the family cooked, ever. I was to outfit the kitchen with all necessaries, adding to the china and serving pieces as I saw fit.

I arrived at the house and met by the house manager who was in the midst of making light fixtures, apparently he did everything but cook for the Toll family. I soon found out that Ira was a jack of all trades and could master all problems. I realized by looking around the kitchen that quite a few appliances were needed for me or for anyone to create a meal so with what I call my master sheet; I knew how to take care of this without too much expense.

Ira spoke with the owner and said that it was apparent to him that I could do the job, especially after viewing my book and giving details over the phone about my foods. There was a housekeeper, Sara, who worked daily, no weekends, so I had no worries as to the cleaning of the kitchen floor but I would of course, keep the counters and appliances clean. This young girl was married with a child and was born in Cuba but raised in the U.S. so for me she was to be a godsend as you will see later.

As soon as the kitchen was organized, I made stocks and then made a few different soups with small versions as tasters, for the couple to try on their arrival. I also made samples of my pastries, as I understood they had a sweet tooth. There was one dish that I had never made and that was chopped liver, a Jewish staple. I had a book on Jewish cooking which I had used quite a lot in my cooking career, so I bought a sample of this spread from the local delicatessen and then proceeded to make mine with Ira being my taster as I perfected, according to him, the perfect chopped liver.

When the couple arrived, I took my bills to the office to be reimbursed as I had paid with my own cash and Mr. Toll took care of them. I persuaded them both to try my taster soup samples and to enjoy my desserts. Well, they went crazy over all my food samples, so I asked for a list of their likes and dislikes. They did not like garlic, so that would be easy enough for me to keep a sprinkle jar in the kitchen for any guests that requested garlic.

I placed a plate with crackers and my homemade liver spread for Mr. Toll, who then took it to his office, as Ira said that he liked to have a nibble between meals. I inquired if he enjoyed my chopped liver and he replied, '"You bought this at the deli as I have seen the bill" and I explained this spread had not been bought, but I had made my own for the first time, and to ask Ira about the experiment, which he did and then apologized since the spread I had bought would not have covered half a dozen crackers.

Oh dear, what had I gone and done? I created a monster by showing off my talent and now was in for much more work than anticipated, because the idea of having parties to showcase their newly renovated home was implanted in their minds. The house was not built by this worldwide builder but bought in Palm Beach where it was renovated to suit their tastes. They had originally owned a home south in Manalapan, a very beautiful area but hit badly by the hurricane two years before, so they relocated to an area in Palm Beach right on the water (not the ocean). In fact, there was always water damage in properties that were on the ocean but no salt water intrusion on lakeside properties.

The Toll's asked me to prepare for a party of twelve guests, of course during my three day a week stay, so the first day was to be preparation time, the next day the party and hopefully the third day would be much easier. I hired a bartender-waiter and one other waiter to handle the front dining room. I set up one of the place settings to show how I wanted it to be done for the party and used Sara to help me in the kitchen. We ended up as quite a team with her soon reading my mind as to how she could help. She became my right hand as I could not do the formal service, dish washing and cleaning by myself. Strange though, how the schedule changed and I found myself doing two parties each week. The first thing I did in the mornings was to make soft creamed eggs topped with caviar that they had brought with them.

Their favorite hors d'oeuvres were English Beef Sausage Rolls, Chicken Liver, Apple, Cream and Cognac Pate en Croute (aspic glazed and served in a water lily napkin) on a silver tray with fresh melba toast and, of course Caviar with Blinis to be passed. I made some of my special cheese straws (recipe included) for their party. Since the guest list was different for every party, thank goodness, this enabled me to do preparation for more than one party at a time, seeing as how I could do the same dishes over and over with no problem. The soup was Mr. Toll's choice but a few times Mrs. Toll asked for a salad style first course like goat cheese crusted with chopped nuts then sizzled in a pan to be served on a bed of baby greens with a balsamic dressing. The favorite Entrée was Roast Filet of Beef in wine sauce. I offered a chicken dish or grilled vegetables with a French mushroom omelet.

Their favorite desserts were silver platters full of my petit pastries to be placed in the center of the table so guests could partake of whatever they so desired. This was a talking point, as many ladies were on diets and they could just have a taste of what we say in England, "A little of what you fancies does you good." At the request of Mr. Toll, now and then I made individual Chocolate Pots du Crème (recipe included) and offered my homemade Chocolate Liqueur Truffles to be passed with coffee to round out the evening.

Well not exactly to round out the evening as earlier when the guests arrived, Mr. Toll had shown them his art collections inside the house and outside on the grounds and as I say this was before dinner and a preamble to the specialty du soir which was to introduce me (with the dog Tracey) to the guests and, of course stressing that I was their personal chef, Pauline Tiffany. The wait staff certainly got their kicks out of this fiasco.

When Mr. Toll said that they wanted to have a party for twenty, I had to put my foot down as I was not a caterer. So, they called in their old caterer and asked me to supervise the proceeding and I said that it would be no problem after all I had been in this business for many years. Mr. Toll had asked his housekeeper Glory, from their home up north, to come down so I could teach her soufflés and soups, so she could do them when they returned home at the end of the season. Apparently Mr. Toll had sent her to a special class to learn how to make soufflés but apparently it did not work, so it was up to me. One problem though, Glory was not interested in learning anything new as she was well taken care of by the family and treated like a guest after being with them for quite a few years.

When she arrived, Glory made herself at home sitting with the family at the counter in the kitchen reading the newspaper and did not want to help in any way or learn any dishes that Mr. Toll had wanted me to teach her. They invited a couple of their closest friends to dinner, where Glory and I were to work together to produce a nice meal followed by a chocolate soufflé. Glory did not lift a finger and I served the meal after cooking it as she watched me prepare the soufflé. I realized that she had no intention of ever making a soufflé. The meal was a hit and I cleaned up after she had filled herself with my cooking. She then retired to the guest cottage to watch TV.

Next day there was to be a party for sixteen guests and I was busy preparing for it. Mr. Toll asked me to come to his office and said that he wanted Glory to help me with the party instead of our housekeeper. I told him that this would not work as Sara knew my ways but he was adamant. I said, "Sir, Glory is too slow and can't possibly keep up with me, so I don't want to use her," to which he said, "Pauline, she is getting old so do have patience with her as I want you to train her and use her." I asked how old Glory was and he said that she was at least sixty five and I said to him, "Sir, I am much older than that and I would never have mentioned it before, but I have had lung cancer. Part of my left lobe has been removed and the whole right lobe, so if I can do all of this, I cannot for the life of me see how she can be so slow, using her age as a factor for not pulling her weight." That was a stunning statement but I had to say it. Mr. Toll then replied that of course I should use Sara and anyone else as I saw fit and then I left his office. A few days later, Glory left.

When there was a party too big for me to handle, I would call the caterer that the Toll's had previously used for parties of four. This caterer was not at all upset that the family no longer called her for small parties, as this was a pain to do and she preferred large parties. Having been a caterer myself, I would not have even considered catering small parties of four.

When the caterers arrived, I placed all my recipes and menus, and my tools of the trade out of sight as I did not wish anyone to misuse my personal knives, etc. The garages were open and ready for them with grills, ovens, stoves and refrigerators ready for their use, even tables for prep work. The caterer had ordered all of this equipment just like I used to do.

What I had not taken into consideration was that they would use the house kitchen. When I was a caterer, I was self contained and would not have dreamed of using the client's kitchen, as people usually wanted to see the kitchen, and especially so, when working for realtors who wanted to show a model house. I had to take my operation out of the kitchen so that it was spick and span for viewing. Not so with this caterer as she forgot the butter, even the coffee and cream so there they were tracking dirt in and out of the kitchen.

The house refrigerators became fair game and the caterers stacked them full of their canapés etc. and never in my catering history had I seen so much chaos. I watched this caterer not in complete charge of her business and I did what was needed to get through whatever it took. It was a charity event and naturally people wanted to see the house, including the kitchen and breakfast room. Ira was always on duty during these catered affairs, to help wherever needed and he was superb.

Restaurant owners kept their best tables reserved for the top tippers and for their status in Palm Beach. Being Rod Stewart guaranteed the best table in the house as the business would surely be mentioned in the Shiny Sheet next day. This was obvious when I booked a table for my old boss and also when I booked a table for myself under the name, Mrs. Tiffany, as explained in previous chapters.

At one of the parties which I catered at the Tolls, Sidney Kimmel and his new wife were invited. I told my employer that I had worked for Mr. Kimmel to get his estate ready for occupancy, but did not think that he would recognize me after all it had been a few years ago and my tenure was short due to politics and left it at that. Well, the party was a great success and as always, I was introduced (with the dog) to the guests and then Mr. Toll looked at Mr. Kimmel and said, "Sidney, Pauline used to work for you but now I have her working for me as my private chef." I was flummoxed at this remark, especially as he brought me forward right next to Mr. Kimmel. I told Mr. Kimmel that I was glad to see him and meet his new wife and he said to me, "I am so sorry but I do not remember you as my memory is not as good as it used to be, but I must say you are one great chef." That was it and all I wanted to do was crawl under the table (with the dog) as after all he had had no knowledge of my dismissal and I had done nothing about it for fear that I might have never worked in Palm Beach again.

The last week in March, Mr. Toll came into the kitchen and told me, "Seeing as how we have met all our social obligations, and you have done such a fantastic job for us, we shall not be requiring your services until next season." You see, the guests who had been entertained at their home would now reciprocate with so many invitations to finish their season with a bang and they hoped that I would return next season. I had no inclination to return because even though the pay seemed great at the beginning, when I figured out the hours and miles on my car   (as no house car was provided) I was working far below scale.

CHEESE STRAWS

Ahead of time, place in a container, 1 cup parmesan cheese shavings, 1 tsp. dry garlic, 1 tsp. dried parsley, 1 tsp. dried chives, 1 tsp. Italian herbs, ½ tsp. salt, ½ tsp. pepper. Refrigerate. Place a sheet of wonton wrapper on a board, brush on melted butter then sprinkle on a good part of the cheese mix. Cut lengthwise into 8 strips, place on parchment paper, and bake 350 degrees., approximately 8-10 minutes. Save in an airtight container, not refrigerated. Can rescrisp carefully if needed. Place on a greased parchment-lined tray. Watch as burns easily.

CHOCOLATE MOUSSE

½ cup milk
3 tbsp. sugar
1 tsp. expresso powder
1 cup bitter chocolate chips
3 egg whites

Heat milk, sugar and expresso powder (not boil). Blend the chocolate chips. Add the milk mixture and egg white. Blend till smooth. (Can add 2 tbsp. rum or coffee liqueur). Pour into individual glass dishes and refrigerate. Top with whipped cream and a fresh mint leaf or grated chocolate.

Chapter
23 EPILOGUE

After I had finished the season for the Toll family, I realized that my health issues would stop me from resuming my chef or management career. I had two large lung surgeries, previously, and now there were some concerns that there were some other problems in the lungs too. So, I called on my friend Jan Fogt (a writer and author), to see if she could advise me on how to write a small book of my life. I talked to her and said maybe I should put down a few of my memoirs that my grandchildren could enjoy; it would be a biography, but I figured it would be very small. So Jan came on over with bunches of paper and she was scribbling like crazy, and of course the good reporter she is, she got down quite a few ideas. As I said, I wanted to document my life in a very small and condensed form. Jan and I worked it seemed for hours, with lots of paper all over the place and I said, "What do you think, Jan?" Her answer was just one thing. She said, "Pauline, you've got a book that needs publishing, not just a small autobiography for the children."

I said, "Jan, I'd love to do this, but I am not a professional writer." I could do a few recipes for the book, and I've done videos, but I did not think I was good enough to write a book. So I said, "Would you do it for me?" She gave me an emphatical answer of, "Pauline, these are your words - your accent with a hint of your colloquial Yorkshirism and expressions. If someone was to try and write this for you, it would not be the same; it would not have the same impact. No, I'll not write this for you. You're going to do it yourself!"

The computer and I were alienated. I had never used one before in my life, so we decided that I'd tape the chapters and my girlfriend, Karel Van Gelder, down in North Palm Beach would transpose them onto her computer. This seemed to do quite well at first, but Karel had too many irons in the fire with her work and being busy as always. So, I said, "Look, I'll go out and buy a good old-fashioned $99 typewriter and proceed on it, like I did all the times in the years before when I wrote recipes, cooking class information and press releases." So, one day Karel came to my house, bringing over the chapters that we had gone through – not finished, of course. There she was, lugging this computer and printer. She set it up on my table (my dining room table), which was now my office desk, and she said, "Sit down there, Pauline, I'm going to teach you some basic computer skills!" Well, you could've knocked my socks off, I swear. I thought "No way I can do this!" But I sat there and started typing.

With trial and error, I managed to do most of the chapters with the help of my son, Paul. I would call him at least twice a day for his expertise, and he came over just about every day (after his stressing day teaching school). I began to notice a sense of "oh dear, not again" in my son's voice, but he took it all in stride. Karel, of course, stopped to see me and check on my progress weekly, bringing some fried chicken from my favorite chicken store so we could "nosh" (eat) whilst working. She got such a kick out of the fact that I craved this Bud's fried chicken (we did not have a store here in Stuart). Donna, my best friend and I were never off the phone; she was the "Aunt" to my children and is mentioned in many of my previous chapters.

My granddaughter, Kristal Bell, (who at age 23 is a schoolteacher, computer whiz, and savvy in deciphering my voice) took a couple of my tapes and did a couple of chapters for me. Then, I had to go through thousands of my recipes that I had used for all the different people I had worked for and lots of photographs to place in the book. (Maybe instead, I should have written, not a book, but like a "photographscape" of all the photographs with captions underneath that would tell the story! That's what I'll do next time! Oh, no way!) There's only one book because there's only one life.

My friend, Suzanne, a spirited eighty-nine year old world-traveler, would come on over and take the chapters from me or I'd take them over to her (she only lived a few doors from me). You see, she was married to the Station Director of Scripps, (of course, Scripps is a big publishing company). I used to give her each chapter and she would critique them for me. Very few people outside of my family knew my story and I believe there were lots of skeptical people who thought I was full of hogwash. I imagine they said to themselves, "Oh yeah, she says she's got this book!" I even started to believe that I wasn't really doing it, but that was the doubting Thomases. The book is finally done, and as they say "I've got to put it to bed!", so readers of my autobiography can enjoy learning about my different lives "above stairs" with the aristocrats and "below stairs" when I was working for the people of Palm Beach.

Many wonderful people took on assignments from my dear friend, Natalie. A couple of high school students, Ariana Martinez and Kara Russell, wanted to help with the book, so they took on a couple of chapters to proof them. Diana Young-Stewart, took on the incredible job of formatting and editing the book! There are not enough thanks, Diana! Another dear friend, Suzanne Huron-Livengood, did a super job on the cover for Natalie. "Smashing! Shall we say! Fabulous job!" I mean these are all fine people, having volunteered their services.

Please understand that most of these recipes in this book are to do with the people in that chapter. It doesn't mean to say that they are not much up to scratch, but it was the type of food that they requested. The other sort of recipes, shall we say "gourmet-style", I show my talents of that in my restaurants and the catering of my gourmet food shop.

Suzanne said to me, "You've got to get on the computer now and get people to write to you and if they need help, they can ask you questions," and I said, "No, I don't think I'd like to do that" – but I don't mind if people call me if they've got a query in my book (or other cooking questions) because that used to happen quite a lot after I did cooking shows on the radio in West Palm Beach, many years before. I would do this radio show, people would call in and ask questions and usually it had nothing pertaining to what we were talking about in the beginning! So the program took on its own character, but that was a lot of fun too, and to see like six telephone lines flashing, all of those waiting to ask me questions or just chat with me, was great.

I'd like to personally acknowledge everybody with gratitude for what they've done to help me, so a special "heartfelt" thank you to my neighbours Jack and Maureen, who would fetch and carry for me when I was sort of "bedridden" for a time. My thanks to my friend, Virginia Mossburg, for support; so much fun to be with in Palm Beach. Thanks also to Tom, the "housekeeper" extraordinaire, for organizing my life as well as cleaning up after me! Both Suzanne and I use his expertise.

A special thank you goes out to Natalie West-Evans, who did more than her share in helping me through all this. This is not the first book she has had a part in publishing, and apparently she said she enjoys doing it. No doubt about it, this is hard work, especially when you are trying to raise a family, you are a Minister's wife, and you are going to school to get your degree as well.

Lastly, special devotion to my children; John, Paul, Tommy and grandchildren, Krystal, Tiffany, Melissa, my T.J. and gorgeous Allana. What a full life I have lead, definitely not boring, full of excitement, emotional intrigue and never a dull moment in this "Perils of Pauline's" life![1]

---

[1] Referring to the 1947 movie called "The Perils of Pauline" starring Betty Hutton